A–Z

OF

BRECON

PLACES - PEOPLE - HISTORY

Mal Morrison

AMBERLEY

First published 2020

Amberley Publishing
The Hill, Stroud, Gloucestershire, GL5 4EP
www.amberley-books.com

Copyright © Mal Morrison, 2020

The right of Mal Morrison to be identified as
the Author of this work has been asserted in
accordance with the Copyrights, Designs and
Patents Act 1988.

ISBN 978 1 4456 9277 7 (print)
ISBN 978 1 4456 9278 4 (ebook)

British Library Cataloguing in Publication Data.
A catalogue record for this book is available
from the British Library.

Typesetting by Aura Technology and Software
Services, India. Printed in Great Britain.

Contents

Introduction

What could I write about the town of Brecon that hadn't previously been covered? This was the question I posed myself when asked to write my fourth book about the town. The answer, I'm happy to say, is quite a lot! Here, right at the very heart of the most beautiful of Britain's national parks, lies our town of contrasts, enigmas and spirits; a town that holds a little place in all of our hearts. We love the charmingly named streets, dripping with charisma and history, and we love the people who made it what it is.

A–Z of Brecon takes the reader on a fascinating and exciting tour through the primary and lesser-known streets and thoroughfares. Along the way we meet famous Breconians; unselfish, ordinary, and sometimes extraordinary people who have given so much to our town.

At the launch of *Secret Brecon* a few years ago, a lady asked if it contained any ghosts. This time I can give a definite YES. We are going to visit some of Brecon's most haunted locations, and expose the spirits lurking within. With so many historic buildings it would be unusual if there were not a few resident spirits around. We recount tales of these ghostly spectres, identifying the buildings where they are reputed to dwell; do they really exist or are they the product of bottled spirits and/or overactive imaginations? You, the reader, can pass judgement.

The Brecon Beacons from Tir-y-groes, Cantref. (Malcolm Morrison)

As our alphabet progresses, we meet visitors and invaders who have settled here over the centuries. We remember the poet who inspired Sassoon and Wordsworth, meet the lady who was without doubt the world's most revered opera singer, and of course the baby born here in our town who became the most famous actress of her time. We meet Brecon ladies we can be proud of; visionary women who were generations ahead of their time and had to overcome jealousy and misogyny to fulfil their goals.

Some very special locations both here in the town and occasionally a little distance away will be visited, recalling events and anecdotes from our fascinating past. When we pass beyond the town walls to recall events from our romantic past we reveal recently discovered artefacts which have lain hidden since the greatest show on earth visited our county. Buildings, walls and bridges may give a town its strength, but it is its people who warm the heart and give it life. Brecon has its share of captivating residents, both living and departed, and many of them will be remembered as we progress through our pretty little town that we love so much. When we eventually reach the twenty-sixth letter of our breathless alphabet, we will perhaps understand a little better who we are and how we came to be here. We are about to walk among some of the greatest Breconians who ever lived; men and women of whom we can be justly proud.

Malcolm Morrison, 2019

Behind the Sgwd yr Eira waterfall, Brecon Beacons National Park. (Malcolm Morrison)

Adelaide Gardens

This pretty housing estate built soon after the end of the Second World War commemorates Miss Adelaide Mary Williams (1850–1942), a daughter of the Williams family of Penpont, one of the most ancient and connected families of the county. She took an active interest in the social issues of her day, especially the working conditions of farm labourers, and was a staunch supporter of the temperance movement. She had a special affection for Llanfaes, founding a detachment of the Boys' Brigade and organising a gymnasium and football team. She was a school governor and in 1895, together with Gwenllian Morgan, was elected a Poor Law Guardian, the first women to hold such office in Brecon.

The good work carried out in Llanfaes by Miss Adelaide Williams is recorded countless times in the press; one account expressed the wish that 'she would be long spared to continue'. Adelaide Williams took great pleasure working with the 'Comrades of the Great War', especially when this included 'her old boys of the Llanfaes Boys' Brigade'.

It is rumoured that the Williams family once bore the name Bullen or Boleyn with connections to the family of Anne Boleyn, whose portrait at Hampton Court Palace is

Above: Adelaide Gardens, 2019. (Malcolm Morrison)

Right: Adelaide Williams. (Richard Williams)

said to bear a striking resemblance to Adelaide Williams. The ancestry link is fairly tenuous but can possibly be traced to a knight from Boulogne during the Norman conquest. The family has, in the past, made a lot of the Boleyn connection, for example naming one of their Brecon properties Boleyn House. It is a nice but unproven link. Adelaide Williams died in 1942.

The Avenue

The Avenue is a short road, part of which seems to have been created during the construction of the railways. Prior to this the road ran into Dainter Street (then known as Baily Glas), where it forked left into Well Street – the site of a well responsible for a particularly nasty cholera epidemic in 1854 – and onwards towards the Mill Street and Cradoc Road junction (known as 'Black Boy' for reasons unknown). Baily Glas continued towards today's Maendu Street (comprising London Row, Priory Row and Nicholas Row), and on towards the Priory.

The Avenue seems to have been created to link the junction at the Cwm Inn/Mill Street with the road from town, avoiding the elevated sections of rail track that scythed through Dainter and Well streets. The scars left by this major construction are still visible.

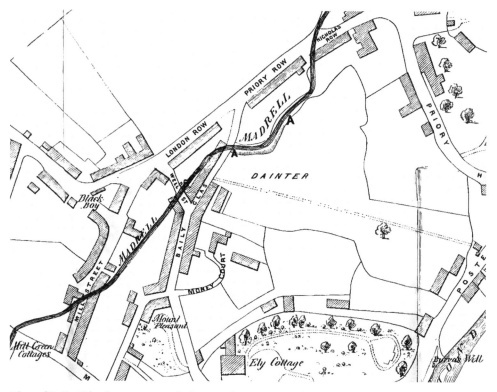

Plan of Baily Glâs, from an 1854 cholera epidemic report. (Roger Barrington)

Alexandra Road, 2019.
(Malcolm Morrison)

Alexandra Road

Alexandra Road is named after Queen Alexandra, the profoundly deaf wife of Edward VII. It contains many impressive Edwardian town houses in a quiet location just a stone's-throw from the town centre. The railway, before its closure, ran along the south-western side of the road; then it was a through road but nowadays it is a quiet cul-de-sac. Alexandra Road's elevated position allows some spectacular views across the town towards the Brecon Beacons and, despite the passing years, it has retained its charm and has some extremely desirable town houses.

Army Connections

Many famous regiments have at one time or another made Brecon their home. During the twentieth century, 24th Regiment connections were everywhere, including a well-supported Old Comrades Club, which was located first in Castle Street before moving to Bridge Street.

Regimental Colours from Isandlwana and other campaigns, Brecon Cathedral. (Malcolm Morrison)

The Parachute Regiment's battle school was once established here but Dering Lines today is a centre of excellence. The Parachute Regiment's time here left a small but significant group of families with regimental connections. Some settled here after army service, others married local girls and remained or returned later. Gurkha soldiers have been based in Brecon for over forty-five years and around eighty Nepalese families have made their homes here with several local enterprises reflecting the connection. In 2019 Brecon town twinned with Dhampus in Nepal. It is this military melting pot that has given Brecon some of its richness and a character that is quite unlike any of its neighbours.

Adelina Patti

Adelina Patti was born in Madrid in 1843 and became the finest opera singer of her era, performing at all of the finest venues throughout Europe and America. During her 1862 American tour, she sang at the White House for President Abraham Lincoln and his wife. The purity and beauty of her voice meant that she could demand huge fees for a single performance and was sometimes paid in gold. Recordings of her voice still exist however; most were made late in her life when the recording equipment was rudimentary to say the least.

In 1878 she purchased Craig-y-Nos Castle in Breconshire where she added a theatre and installed a billiard table, a game she loved. Here she staged private performances to friends and visitors and made frequent visits to Brecon. She regularly attended events in Brecon including the 1889 Eisteddfod, arriving by train (the Eisteddfod field was in Cerrigcochion Road). On 24 May 1897 she was made an honorary burgess of the town and presented with a scroll in a casket made of oak taken from the roof of the cathedral in recognition of her eminent and munificent services to the poor of Brecon. Undoubtedly a world superstar of her day, she died at Craig-y-Nos in 1919 and is buried in Paris in accordance with her wishes. At the time of writing, several events are being planned in the county to commemorate the centenary of her death.

Adelina Patti by Franz Winterhalter, 1862.

B

Bridge Street

The first building in Bridge Street is the former Old White Lion Inn, later known as the Bridgend Inn. Standing downstream on the Llanfaes side of the Usk Bridge, the former inn is currently part of the Christ College complex. A local gentleman recalls a tale his father often told regarding leaving the inn in the small hours. He was surprised by the ghostly figure of a monk walking through the reception area. As he approached, the figure turned and looked at him before walking away. Today the roof of the building seems to have been adopted by a large colony of pigeons, they don't appear to be 'spooked'.

There once was a short terrace in Dinas Road called White Lion Terrace, later renamed Dinas Row. It suffered miserably from the flooding that once plagued this part of town, and eventually had to be demolished. Nowadays flooding is a rarity, but it was not just Dinas Road that suffered; Bridge Street regularly flooded during the winter months, as did Orchard Street and Silver Street. During the days before a proper sewerage system served Llanfaes, it is recorded that it was flooding by the river that took away the filth that accumulated on the streets. Drainage in Llanfaes, due to its flatness, was far more difficult than in other parts of town. A drainage ditch ran the length of Orchard Street and Bridge Street on the college side of the street but was incapable of meeting its needs. It came in for considerable criticism in a report into the sewerage, drainage and supply of water and the sanitary conditions of the inhabitants of Brecon in 1849.

The Bridgend Hotel, Llanfaes, *c.* 1950. (Andrew Williams)

Bridge Street, Llanfaes. (Malcolm Morrison)

Bell Lane

Bell Lane, like many of Brecon's streets, got its name from a large coaching inn that stood at its junction with High Street Superior. Today much of the area is derelict and desperately in need of some tender loving care and some sympathetic restoration. Few Breconians can remember the Bell Inn being open, but it had stabling for many horses back in the day, and its 'Great Room' welcomed artistes and travelling shows. Sarah Siddons and her parents' company, 'The Strolling Players', performed here several times, as well as at other locations in the town. We are fairly sure that her husband to be proposed to her right here in the Bell Inn, much to the horror of her parents.

The buildings that once comprised the Bell Hotel (2019). (Malcolm Morrison)

Tractor Boys at Brecon Show, Newton Park, *c.* 1958. (Andrew Williams)

Brecon Show

Brecon Show is the oldest agricultural show in Britain, founded in March 1755. The first secretary was Mr John Harper of the Golden Lion, Brecon, the first president Charles Powell of Castle Madoc (elected 16April 1755). Its original home is believed to have been at Newton Park with the show usually taking place in mid-September. Its bi-centenary show was held on Saturday 6 August 1955 and was honoured by the presence of the newly crowned Queen Elizabeth II. The Queen, and approximately 200 invited guests, enjoyed a luncheon that included Usk salmon, Brecknockshire lamb, fresh fruit salad and cream and Brecknock cheese with Brecknockshire Farm butter and biscuits.

Brecon Barracks

Brecon Barracks, located in the Watton, was originally built in 1805 and is currently home to 160 (Wales) Brigade. The Keep, built for the storage of arms and ammunition, was added in 1879. The 24th Regiment, famous for their role in the Zulu Wars, once made their headquarters here and, although they now form part of the Royal Welsh

'A' Company, 24th Foot Re-enactment Group, The Watton, 2019. (Andrew Williams)

Regiment, the association continues. The Regimental Museum holds artefacts from many campaigns including the defence of Rorke's Drift. The Royal Welsh now operates as the lead armoured infantry task force in the British army.

Brecon Beacons

The Brecon Beacons are the iconic mountains that stand silently watching over the town. The great peak, Pen y Fan, is the highest in South Wales, accompanied by the table of Corn Ddu and the knife-edged Cribyn. The three peaks are instantly recognisable and just seeing them daily lets the people of Brecon know that they are home.

The Bulwark

The Bulwark is a large triangular area in the centre of town incorporating St Mary's Church and the iconic statue of the Duke of Wellington. I suppose it could be said that the Bulwark is the heart of Brecon. Here the biannual fairs are located, invoking charters that are centuries old and thwarting attempts to move the mediaeval biannual event to a site away from the town centre.

The Bulwark from High Street, 2019. (Malcolm Morrison)

The Bulwark from Watton Mount, 2019. (Malcolm Morrison)

Bethel Square

Bethel Square is a modern shopping precinct between Lion Street and the central car park. It gained its name from Bethel Chapel, which was once the largest place of worship in the area with seating for over 800 souls. It is also the site of the Golden Lyon Inn that gave Lion Street and Lion Yard their names. Another chapel, Dr Cokes, stood nearby on land now occupied by the Co-op supermarket. The Plough Chapel is the only one remaining of the three Lion Street chapels.

Bethel Square, 2019. (Malcolm Morrison)

Castles

Wales is assumed to have the largest number of castles per square mile in the world and Brecon can boast three very differing fortifications. The earliest, Pen-y-crug, dates from the Iron Age and the surviving earthworks give a good impression of its size and strength. The Roman fortress at Y Gaer dates from the second century and portions of its stone walls and gatehouses remain. In fact, due to surveys and recent excavations we seem to know more about this fortress than about the more recent Norman castle.

Brecon Castle. (Malcolm Morrison)

Brecon Castle

Brecon Castle was originally a motte-and-bailey built by the Norman invader Neufmarché in the eleventh century. It evolved into an imposing stone fortification around which the walled town of Brecon grew, but no one really knows how Brecon's castle looked at the height of its importance. There are no accurate drawings, although John Speed's plan of 1610 and Meredith Jones' of 1744 do provide us with a rough idea. Surprisingly little archaeological work has been carried out on the site, but it is believed that there were two main entrances and a postern gate. The main gate faced west overlooking the ford across the River Usk. It was entered by a drawbridge, probably guarded by semicircular towers, a great door and portcullis. Entry from the town would have been via a drawbridge across the Honddu River into today's Castle Street. The site was encircled by a curtain wall, enclosing the whole castle and its environs. The actual location of the Postern Gate is not known but was likely somewhere near the old Postern Gaol. The imposing Great Hall, which is now part of the Castle of Brecon Hotel, may have formed part of this curtain wall, which probably enclosed today's Bishop's Palace and its grounds. The castle had a chapel dedicated to St Nicholas, and the usual array of kitchens, stables and, we believe, a 30-foot-deep well. It came under attack from the Welsh several times; at least three of these assaults were successful (1215, 1264 and 1265).

Edward Stafford, Duke of Buckingham, was born here at Brecon Castle in 1478. He rose to become one of the most powerful men in the country serving Henry VII and Henry VIII. It was he who built the iconic Buckingham Tower at St Mary's Church, which dominate Brecon's skyline, but, like his father before him, he was charged with high treason, and at Tower Hill on 17 May 1521, went to the executioner's block.

In the Spring of 1648, rebellion broke out in Wales and other parts of the country, and Parliament sent Oliver Cromwell to put it down. The rebel forces were subsequently

The Buckingham Tower, St Mary's. (Malcolm Morrison)

defeated by an army under Colonel Horton, who had marched from Brecon in severe weather. Whilst it is rumoured that Cromwell himself ordered the destruction of the castle at Brecon, there seems to be no evidence that he ever came here; however, it was at this time that the castle and the town's walls were destroyed. Brecon was known for its royal support and the parliamentary armies would have been quite aware of this.

The Castle Hotel, which incorporates much of the castle remains, is reputed to have a resident ghost known as Lucy. Several people claim to have encountered her; one lady refused to go along a corridor to her room because she could feel the ghostly presence. Other stories mention a grey lady seen walking the corridors in older parts of the building, past the kitchens and toilets.

Cathedral

The cathedral, once known as the Priory Church of St John the Evangelist, was originally a Benedictine priory founded around 1093 by the Norman Neufmarché. It has been rebuilt, much restored and extended over the centuries but monastic use ceased at the dissolution of the sixteenth century.

Above: Brecon Cathedral from the Tythe Barn, 2019. (Andrew Williams)

Left: Brecon Cathedral from the Lych Gate, 2019. (Malcolm Morrison)

The Games family of Brecon owe their fame and fortune to their traditional support for the monarchy. During the Civil War Charles I was welcomed here with his forces and stayed overnight at Priory House as the guest of Sir Herbert Price, governor of the town and the castle. Local people supplied horses enabling his soldiers to continue their journey the next day. It is little wonder that the parliamentary army were a little upset by this and the priory came in for special attention from Cromwell's army. We know that certain monuments within the building were damaged and special attention was given to a memorial to members of the Games family. The carving known as the 'armless lady' is the only surviving piece of what must have been an impressive monument.

By the early eighteenth century the priory was mainly frequented by the poorer population and was in a state of some dilapidation. The windows were glazed, the walls whitewashed, the pews and bells in good order, 'and all things kept as becometh the House of God'. However, the cost of carrying out repairs to the building was prohibitive. Restoration work was eventually carried out, and in 1923 it became the Cathedral for the Diocese and seat of the Bishop of Swansea and Brecon.

A few minutes spent in the yard will be rewarded with some very interesting monuments. Look out for the grave of the holder of the Victoria Cross, a memorial to a soldier accidentally shot during rifle practice on Battle Hill in 1855 and a French prisoner who died here during the Napoleonic Wars. They are relatively easy to find.

In a glass case near the cathedral entrance are the signatures of some famous visitors: the Queen; Archbishop Robert Runcie and Matt Smith, the eleventh Doctor Who and his assistant Amy Pond (who give their address as 'The Tardis'). Nearby is a chapel dedicated to the illustrious 24th Regiment, where its regimental colours, including some from the Zulu Wars, are laid up. Also look out for a relic of Agincourt, a stone on which Cordwainers from Brecon sharpened their arrows, along with many other items of interest awaiting you within the cathedral.

Christ College

Christ College incorporates some of Brecon's oldest buildings, so perhaps we should not be surprised to learn that it also reputedly has its ghosts. It is rumoured that a friar was murdered in the former Dominican friary in the year 1335. Bishop Lucy was involved with the school in the later part of the seventeenth century and his ghost is said to haunt the college, particularly its ancient chapel. He is described on his monument as a 'shining star of the Anglican Church', others remember him as a vengeful persecutor. Lucy is popularly blamed for pranks rather than actual sightings, but the apparition of a ghostly figure has been reliably reported in the sixth form common room – the Venerable Lucy?

A distinguished soldier, author and former college pupil recalls experiencing a psychotic event during a very dark period of his life during which he was taken to

Christ College from Dinas Road, 2019. (Malcolm Morrison)

Communion by Bishop Lucy and given Mass by a wonderful presence. The miraculous event took place towards the end of the twentieth century and rescued the gentleman from his lowest ebb.

Canal

These days the canal area is purely recreational; an area to walk, cycle or take a leisurely ride on a canal barge. Back in the day, roads were extremely poor and although canal construction required huge investment, they provided a reliable and economical method of moving goods in and out of the county. The 30-foot-wide and 33-mile-long Brecon and Abergavenny Canal transformed industry and transport, linking the mainly agricultural Brecon with industrial Monmouthshire. The cutting of the canal commenced in 1796 and on 24 December 1800, the first barge of coal arrived at Brecon; the massive project was completed in 1804. A junction with the Monmouthshire canal was completed in 1811. One can imagine the barges drawn by horses bringing their cargoes of coal, iron ore, timber and limestone from South Wales; a network of horse-drawn tram roads connecting nearby towns and villages.

The canal basin, July 2019. (Malcolm Morrison)

Canal bridge near Conway Street, 2019. (Malcolm Morrison)

Huge quantities of goods were moved both in and out of the town. In its heyday there were twelve wharfs working in Brecon alone.

The canal is fed by water taken from the River Usk near Mill Street, where a large weir stretches diagonally for around 200 yards across the river to the bank opposite the promenade boathouse. Originally the canal commenced just below the Captains Walk and many of the streets off the Watton were themselves canal wharfs. However, much has changed, and the canal now begins at Theatr Brycheiniog, an area to relax and enjoy the quiet ambience.

Captains Walk

There is an urban myth that the Captains Walk footpath was originally an exercise area for French officer prisoners incarcerated here during the Napoleonic Wars. Whilst it is true that French prisoners were sent to Brecon during the Napoleonic Wars, there is no further truth in the story.

The Captains Walk follows the outer town wall from the Watton Mount to the Usk riverbank and was the brainchild of a Captain Thomas Phillips, who became extremely rich transporting slaves from the Gold Coast in Africa to America. Phillips, and his ship *The Hannibal*, are remembered for a particularly controversial voyage in 1694. The slaves were handcuffed to one another in pairs by their wrists and legs and branded with the letter 'H'. When the ship reached Barbados just 372 of the 692 slaves had survived the voyage. The placing of a plaque commemorating Phillips on the Captains Walk caused much controversy as to its appropriateness when it was commissioned by the town council in 2010. We seem to have a penchant for distancing ourselves from unsavoury periods in our history, but we cannot rewrite the past and neither should we forget it. We can only pray that we learn from it.

The new (2019) landscaped Captains Walk is the work of the Rich Brothers (Harry and David), two renowned Brecon-born garden designers who understand the ethos

The new Captains Walk, designed by the Rich Brothers, 2019. (Malcolm Morrison)

of the town. This is a far cry from the featureless tarmacadamed path that it replaces. Now it has pretty floral features and a winding path, which will make this area a lovely feature for resident and visitor alike when it reopens to the public.

Camden Road

The road that was to become Camden Road is clearly marked on an 1834 map of Brecon but is undeveloped and unnamed. By 1904 the road, still apparently without a name, is quite well developed with Bowen Terrace and several impressive town houses along its length as far as the Congregational Memorial College and Sunny Bank. Just when it became Camden Road is a little unclear, but I guess it was around the time that the railway station located here. Much land in the Brecon area was owned by the Marquis of Camden in the early nineteenth century including lands at today's Pendre

Camden Road and the railway embankment, July 2019. (Malcolm Morrison)

and the whole of the Priory. He also held extensive lands north of today's Maendu Street and farms in the Cantref area. In 1834 the Marquess would have been George Charles Pratt, whose impressive titles included 2nd Marquis of Camden, 3rd Earl Camden, 2nd Earl of Brecknock, 3rd Viscount Bayham and 3rd Baron Camden. Quite a titled member of the aristocracy and a notable politician with lands in Kent. The first Marquess had married Elizabeth Jeffreys of The Priory, Brecon.

Camden Road today has some very nice terraced and town houses. The first part of the road is only developed on the northern side opposite the old railway track. The now closed Camden Arms in the Watton is another reminder of the Pratt family's Brecon connection.

Church Lane

Church Lane is a short backstreet that runs from Wheat Street towards St Mary's Church, linking with the inappropriately named Steeple Lane. Apart from the rear entrances of the buildings of High Street and a few Victorian commercial buildings, there is little of interest here. It was in a small inn that backs onto this insignificant street that one of the world's most famous actresses was born.

Sarah Siddons' birthplace, 2019. (Malcolm Morrison)

Demographics

The population of the borough of Brecon in 1831 was recorded as 5,026. Ten years later it had risen to 5,708, made up as follows: St Mary's, 1,945; St John's, 1,832; St David's, 1,300; the Castle, 33; the College, 104; and the Barracks, 494. The population by 2001 is recorded as 7,901 increasing to 8,250 at the 2011 census and estimated to be 8,419 in 2017 with females (4,318) outnumbering males (4,101). The largest age group was the 10–19 years group numbering 1,106; they were closely followed by the 60–69 age group who numbered 1,087. Most other groups numbered around 950 except 70–79 whose numbers were in decline at 824 and 80+ falling to 610. Passport holders: UK passports, 5,818; EU, 212; other, 451; 1,826 residents did not hold a passport.

Religious groups: Christian, 4,847; Hindu, 219; Buddhist, 153; Muslim, 27; Sikh, 8; Jewish, 6; and other, 37. A surprising 2,265 stated they were of no religion.

Dainter Street

The area above the Postern and another near Mount Street were once known as 'Ddeintir'. These were areas where sheets of flannel, from a local factory, were stretched on tenterhooks to dry. Dainter Street takes its name from the larger of these

Dainter Street, formerly known as Baily Glas. (Malcolm Morrison)

areas. This quaint little pedestrianised street was originally known as Baily Glas, which indicates a green enclosure. The short street off it is Well Street, the location of the well where local people drew their water supply; this was grossly polluted with raw sewage from a nearby stream that led to a worrying outbreak of Typhoid during the nineteenth century. The stream (the Madrill) has long been diverted into a culvert.

Davies, Richard

Richard Davies, Archdeacon of Brecon from 1777 to 1859, is described as one of the most remarkable men of his time. The archdeacon was a man of considerable means, the third member of his family with the same name to hold similar office. We know that he owned at least two houses in Brecon – a large town house in Glamorgan Street and another in Lion Street (both locations being very fashionable at the time). He also owned a walled garden near the canal and a large field known as Clawdd y Gaer (Castle Ditch), which today comprises almost all of the car parking and supermarket areas that once housed Brecon's cattle market. He lived at The Archdeaconry, Brecon, and is also recorded as living at Brecon House in the Cathedral Close, the home of the archdeacons of Brecon. Could these have been the same place?

He was an extremely generous man and was also able to tap into the generosity of others. He initiated numerous schemes to alleviate the lives of the poor of Brecon, especially during hard times. In 1820 he obtained a sum of nearly £196, which was distributed to the poor in the form of coal, bread and blankets. On another occasion, when heavy snow had left many of the poor people without employment, he paid from his own pocket for them to clear the snow from the streets of Brecon, and on a similar occasion he found work for them in whitewashing houses and making drains.

Another story tells of the archdeacon who, finding a man in bed while his wife was washing clothes, discovered that his only shirt was in the wash. He went back home and brought back some of his own shirts for the man. The next day his servant found he had no clean shirt to offer his master.

The archdeacon travelled in a carriage drawn by three horses, owned a boat, and employed a manservant named John Fortunatus, believed to have been of Maori

The Chapter House, Brecon Cathedral. (Malcolm Morrison)

decent. Fortunatus had been rescued from a small boat in the sea near Java and is described as an excellent servant. The Archbishop held the rank of major in the local militia and one writer commented on his extremely smart turnout. He accompanied the Brecon militia to Fishguard in 1797 following the botched French invasion; their duties were to guard the prisoners. His sermons included thanksgiving for the victories at Trafalgar, Waterloo and Leipzig; he also claimed that it was he who first suggested the erection of the memorial to General Picton at Carmarthen.

In his later years Davies acquired a different reputation. Some mornings the archdeacon would rise before four and walk 10 miles before breakfast. One lady said he was 'a handsome old man but rather eccentric'. A member of the clergy wrote 'he was at times somewhat more than eccentric; one might say deranged'. The curate of St Mary's complained to the bishop in 1854 that the people would not come to the service if the archdeacon was to take the communion service and others walked out if he preached. The archdeacon had become quite odd, one day bursting with energy and extravagant plans and the next spending all day in bed reading novels. Sometimes he would be carried from room to room on a sofa rather than get up.

Archdeacon Davies was undoubtedly succumbing to a form of mental illness and perhaps should be remembered for his strengths and achievements before he became ill. His benevolence, generosity and his work caring for the poor and needy should never be forgotten by the people of Brecon. Historian Jonathan Williams of Trallong states that Davies and the Williams families of Penpont and Abercamlais were linked by marriage in ways too complicated to explain (or indeed fully understand!).

Dinas Training Home for Orphan Girls

Dinas Training Home for Orphan Girls at Dinas Road, Brecon, was established in 1882 by the Girls' Friendly Society. The home could house up to eight girls aged six to twelve years who were trained for eventual employment in domestic service. A payment of five shillings a week was requested for each girl, although some free cases were also taken in.

On 14 September 1882, the home was accredited as a Certified School, allowing it to receive girls boarded out by the Guardians who administered poor relief and the workhouse system. The running of the establishment was taken over by the Waifs and Strays Society in 1909 and became known as Dinas Orphanage for Girls. This was one of the society's smallest homes, accommodating ten children, but it was well established and maintained by the local community before the society took it over. Mrs Maybery, the Honorary Secretary, commented that the home was 'beautifully situated' and that the 'children thrive well'.

The home ran a strict routine whereby the eldest girl carried out most of the housework and laundry while the other children attended school. In dark winter evenings the girls would spend two nights a week on their needlework, all helping to make what matron called their 'special objects'. Other events in the home included the weekly evening service when the girls were taught how to sing in chorus and learnt passages from the Bible. Sunday evening was always set aside as 'story night'.

The 1891 census records thirty-eight-year-old Miss Harriet Fennell as its matron; six boarders are listed: Edith Sage (14) and her sister Eliza Mary Sage (11), both born in Sutton in Surrey; Fanny Elizabeth Fisher (13) and her sister Adelaide Maud Fisher (7) born in Swindon; Charity Ellen Sabine (13) born in London and a local girl, Catherine Dennison (3), born in Llanfrynach.

A later resident, known only as 'J', was an illegitimate child born 25 July, 1883 in Marylebone, London. Both her parents had died, her mother from complications during childbirth and her father (a shoemaker) of bronchitis. She had no known relations apart from her three younger sisters, who it is believed were living at a Dr Barnardo Home. She had an adult half brother and sister, but her parents had never married. The legitimate daughter had taken care of the younger children while her father was ill but since his death, could not take care of them. The child 'J' was taken in by a couple who cared for her for three years but were unable to keep her, because of the foster mother's failing health. She was received at the Dinas Orphanage, Brecon, in May 1894. In December 1899 'J' was placed in service as an under-housemaid. What became of her? We shall probably never know.

In 1901 the matron was a Ruth Hedley, aged forty-eight, from Todmorton in Yorkshire and the census recorded eight boarders: Eva Jones (8) from Builth; Ada Priddice (13) from London; Marion Morgan (13) and sister Mable Morgan (8) from Hay-on-Wye; Clara Murray (10), born Canterbury, Kent; Mary Dobbyn (11), born in Swindon; Annie Bailey (6), born in Mansfield; and Ethel Tadrick (8), who was born in India but is listed as a British subject.

One Sunday night near Christmas 1917, a new arrival to the home caused a quite a commotion. Upon entering the home, the new resident immediately flew upstairs and hid in the chimney place. Eventually they coaxed the troublemaker out – it was a cat they had asked for to keep the mice down!

Dinas Lodge, formerly the Dinas Training Home for Orphan Girls, 2019. (Malcolm Morrison)

Form for admission to Dinas Orphanage by the Waifs and Strays Society.

It is fascinating that most of the boarders came from towns so far away; I feel they were probably quite fortunate not having to suffer the workhouse and it seems that the young ladies were trained to have useful occupations when they matured. How many descendants of these ladies still reside in the town or district? There are photographs in existence showing the children on a visit to the seaside, and it is clear that they were very well cared for and prepared for adult life in Victorian times. It would appear that life at the Dinas Orphanage was good and kept many a young child out of the dreaded workhouse, training them instead for work in the great houses of the county. The orphanage closed in 1918. It remains a beautiful location today.

E

Elston, Harold

Harold Elston was a man of vision; a brilliant entrepreneur and businessman perhaps best remembered for his motor trade business. He had remarkable vision and realised how electricity would change the world. By the year 1925 parts of Brecon had an electricity supply via Mr Elston's privately owned hydro-powered generators in the Struet. It is recorded that he was supplying thirty-three consumers with, he claimed, 100 per cent efficiency.

Elston also pioneered television and wireless. In Brecon in 1931 he received some of the earliest television broadcasts from Crystal Palace. Radio also fascinated him, and he made and sold over 3,500 radio sets, known as 'Elstonphone'. Truly a great Brecon pioneer and entrepreneur.

Harold Elston, man of vision, taken in 1927.

Remains of the East Gate at Watton Mount. (Malcolm Morrison)

East Gate

Brecon town had four gatehouses when it was a walled town: Watergate, West Gate, Struet Gate and East Gate. Part of one of the towers of the East Gate at the Watton Mount has survived the centuries but little evidence of the others survives except for the foundations of the West Gate that were uncovered during a road improvement scheme and marked with road studs near the Usk Bridge.

St Eluned

St Eluned (aka St Aled) was a daughter of Brychan, the ancient King of Brycheiniog. She was martyred in the fifth century and many stories of her life survive. A Holy Well, which had miracles associated with it, lay at the place of her martyrdom on Slwch Tump. The well and the chapel have all but disappeared but accounts of miracles on her feast day (1 August) are recorded. People travelled considerable distances to pray to the blessed virgin to restore their health. Like so many other holy shrines, St Eluned's Well and chapel were damaged during the Reformation.

F

Farming

The production of lamb and beef probably accounts for the lion's share of farming in Breconshire. Dairy and arable farming are important to local agriculture but, currently, sheep rule the hillsides. The Brecon Beacons can be a tough environment for the even most hardy animals to survive, so adult ewes will generally be brought down from the mountain slopes to the lowlands to have their lambs. Normally they are taken back to the hills with their young lambs in late April or early May and gathered down for shearing at the end of June when they and their lambs receive a health check before returning to the hillside. The next time they are brought down is towards the end of July for weaning. The lambs will be kept down while their mothers are returned to the hillsides.

Around September or October, the ewes will be brought down again to mate. After tupping, some return to the hill until the weather turns bad and some farmers send their ewe lambs to winter in warmer climes where they can prosper and grow. They return in April, and after a week or so are taken back to their traditional grazing land on the hills of the Brecon Beacons where they are left to roam. They will remember having been up there with their mothers the previous summer and will have learnt where their stint or heft (area of hill) is and rarely wander far from it during their lifetime.

Many farmers use quad bikes for the round-up (or the 'gather' as it is known). Here we see Dewi, Meirion and Richard Rees, who farm in the Brecon area using horses for the gather.

Sheep gather off the hillside near Brecon. (Wynne Rees)

French POWs

French officers were sent to Brecon during the Napoleonic Wars where they were paroled. It is believed that around eighty-six French officers spent time in Brecon. They were at liberty to walk the turnpike roads for up to 1 mile from the gates of the town but had to return to their lodgings under curfew, which was 5 o'clock during winter and 8 o'clock during the summer months.

The prisoners, it is believed, relied quite a lot upon the charity of the local community and some became quite popular with local people. One painted watercolour pictures of the town, and the Brecknock museum holds examples of this, and other prisoners' work. One prisoner died whilst paroled here and it seems that his headstone was paid for by local people. The plot of the novel *Brecon Adventure* by William Glynne Jones, published in 1951, is centered around his grave in the cathedral yard.

Fringe Festival

As well as its jazz festival, Brecon has developed an alternative free Fringe Festival that provides live music throughout the town. Many of the pubs and cafés stage music events that promote local talent throughout the festival period. The alternative venues feature blues, rock and traditional music to complement the jazz venues. The concurrent events produce a lively and friendly atmosphere throughout the town for the duration of the festival.

The Hours Café and Bookshop, Fringe Festival 2018. (Malcolm Morrison)

Ffynnon Dewi

Ffynnon Dewi roughly translates as St David's fountain or well. The waters still run, producing a good steady flow, but hold no holy traditions that I am aware of. The location is a little obscure, emerging from the bank at the foot of the old Brecon Workhouse hidden behind a row of garages just behind the housing estate that adopted the name of the fountain. It is marked on old maps as a spout, which is correct, but the waters nowadays run into a pipe near its source. The well can be added to the list of Brecon's ancient wells but is not really worth a special visit unless part of a tour of ancient wells in the area.

Free Street

Free Street is a short street at the foot of Cerrigcochian Road. Cerrig Cochian roughly translates into red rocks, a feature at the start of the lane near the summit of the hill that leads to Slwch Tump. Free Street has a little brother, an even shorter and narrower lane called Little Free Street that links it to the Watton. Free Street was formerly known as Heol Rhydd on early town plans but was the primary road that led from the town to its joint railway station in Camden Road.

Free Street (on bin day) looking towards Cerrigcochian Road, 2019. (Malcolm Morrison)

Games Hospital

The Games Hospital is a small terrace in Llanfaes known locally as the Almshouses. It is managed by one of Brecon's oldest surviving charities, beginning life with an indenture dated 1721. Funds and land were gifted by Elizabeth Walker and Katherine Games to provide housing for 'the most ancient and poor women of local parishes', with St Mary's and St David's parishes being preferred. Katherine Games also gave £300 in 1724 to purchase lands whose rents were to pay 40 shillings annually to a charity school for girls; the remainder to be used to distribute bread to the poor.

Originally the hospital, dated 1720, housed twelve sisters (as they were known), who each occupied one room and a small garden for life. Each sister was expected to attend St David's Church every Sunday and holiday or forfeit sixpence. They took turns to attend their fellows who were sick or weak; at Christmas each sister was presented with a gown of coarse woollen cloth by the trustees.

The Games Hospital, better known as the Almshouses, Llanfaes, 2019. (Malcolm Morrison)

By 1873 the entire property had become dilapidated and in 1876 a comfortable and ornamental block was built in its place. It was found necessary to reduce the number of dwellings to six (which in modern times has been further reduced to four). Currently there are five trustees, three of whom are reverend gentlemen, the others having strong Brecon connections. The charity appears to be in sound financial health and the properties are well maintained with pretty gardens in front. Does the charity still own the lands gifted in the indenture?

Guildhall (Town Hall)

A Town Hall or Guildhall has occupied the same site for many years. The first town hall that we have information about was a two-storey wooden structure, built in 1623/4 by John Abel, a carpenter who is credited with several other ornamented half-timbered constructions. Abel was a renowned craftsman who was granted the title 'King's Carpenter' by Charles I for his work during the siege of Hereford. The two-storey timber town hall comprised a ground-floor area containing a courtroom, the area behind being the Council Chamber where the charter, seals and papers of the town were kept. The upper rooms contained a magazine reported to contain arms for

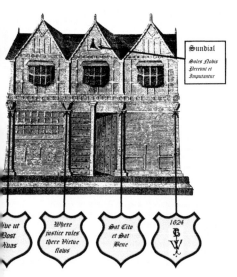

Above: The John Abel wood-built Town Hall, erected in 1624 (replaced in 1771).

Right: BBC reporters at the Guild Hall, election day, July 2019. (Malcolm Morrison)

200 horse and foot. A sundial was fixed on the middle gable carrying the inscription '*Soles Nobis Pereunt et Imputantur*'. This roughly translates as 'We lost and counted suns', a quotation from the Roman poet Martial that appears on several other clocks and sundials including the astronomical clock at Exeter Cathedral.

Four shields adorned the wooden columns on the front of the building. The mottos upon the shields from left to right read '*Vive ut post vivas*' – 'Live your life to the fullest'; 'Where justice rules, there Virtue flows', and '*Sat Cito et Sat Bene*' – Soon enough, but well enough' (reputed to be a quotation from St Jerome). The fourth displayed the date 1624.

By 1770 a replacement for Abel's building was needed, and Andrew Maund was engaged to build it on the same site. In February 1771 it was reported that 'workmen had begun to lay the foundations of a new Town Hall at Brecon which, when finished, will be the gentlest and most complete piece of architecture of this kind in the Principality'. This evolved into today's Guildhall. In the early nineteenth century the building housed an armoury, a market hall and a courtroom. The ground floor comprised the market hall, the arches of which have since been built in, however the basement is thought to date from the 1620s. Renovations completed in 1888 gave the form which we see today including a magnificent Council Chamber on the ground floor and theatre on the first floor, which was renamed the Adelina Patti Theatre in 2019. An intricate ornamental staircase is just one of many features worthy of note in this wonderful old building.

Ghost-hunts have been held in the Guildhall in recent years and video films placed on the YouTube platform by people who participated. These films suggest that they got to talk to some of the spirits in the ancient building. A gentleman responsible for stage lighting in the hall was often in the building alone setting up the lighting computer. On one occasion he took his four-year-old son with him. It was always a spooky place to work, he recalls, and on this particular day, in the dark, he noticed that the racked seating seemed to be quite noisy, which he put down to wind blowing. Later when they arrived home, the young lad told his mother 'There was someone else in the Guildhall with us, but I didn't tell Dad!'

Green Dragon

The Green Dragon in High Street Superior is an interesting building that replaced an earlier inn. The building once housed the offices of the *Brecon County Times,* the predecessor of our beloved *Brecon and Radnor Express*. The printing presses were located in a draughty room at the back of the building, and two shops at the front sold music and confectionery.

In 1891 a Magdalen Davies was running a coffee tavern here. As a teenager this lady had been a general servant for Brecon County Gaol's governor. During the First World War, Mrs Davies catered for events to entertain wounded soldiers. Post Office staff held

The Green Dragon, Market Hall entrance, High Street Superior, *c.* 1895.

their annual supper and social event at the Green Dragon in January 1918 when, for the first time, women were employed as the war had created a shortage of postal workers. Magdalen Davies lost her son, Ivor, in 1918, killed by machine-gun fire in France. The first floor of the building became home to the Brecon Royal Air Force Association branch and the Brecon squadron of the Royal Observer Corps between 1952 to 1971, before it relocated to the former Angel Hotel in the Struet.

Gasworks

The first attempt to light the town by gas was made in 1822 and by 1840 the market house was illuminated by fifty-three gas lights. In 1870 the Brecon Gas Company was supplying an estimated 500 homes and 141 public lamps. The price of gas in 1884 was four shillings and seven pence per thousand feet (with seven pence per thousand discount). The town's gasworks was located on the river side of the canal bank and consisted of a coking plant and two gasometers. Coke, the by-product of coal gas production, was sold at seventeen shillings and sixpence a ton in 1913. Coal gas was replaced by natural gas in the later part of the 1960s, making the gasworks redundant, and soon after, it was demolished. The lane leading to the gasworks kept its name (Gasworks Lane) and these days leads to the canal bank and the Rich Field, home of Brecon's football team.

The gasometer on the canal bank in the Watton. (Adrian Gillard)

Glamorgan Street

Glamorgan Street runs along the south-westerly perimeter of the old town where some fragments of the town walls remain (only visible from the Captains Walk). Some of Brecon's best houses were situated here, but in recent years many of the ornate and larger buildings have seen changes of use. The convent schools were located in some of them, and the town's first museum was originally located here in a converted chapel. Amongst the more interesting of the remaining buildings, and well worth a few moments of our time, are those that make up Buckingham Place, a late sixteenth-century building that was once the home of Brecon and Wales's first lady mayor, Gwenllian Morgan, a heroic lady who faced animosity and misogyny – as we shall read later.

Glamorgan Street looking towards Buckingham Place, 2019. (Malcolm Morrison)

H

High Street

Brecon has the unusual feature of having two High Streets, one named High Street Superior, the other High Street Inferior. The distinction between the two appears to lie in their relative proximity to the castle, with the superior streets being closest. High Street Inferior is by far the grandest and, together with the Bulwark, are generally considered to be the town's main streets. A magnificent triple gas lamp and drinking water fountain installed by former Mayor Alderman William Games *c.* 1890 stood proudly in the triangle in front of Lloyds Bank; it was, with great difficulty, removed many years ago – a horrible mistake many people feel. Both High Streets have some interesting old buildings to check out.

The Games triple gas lamp and drinking fountain, removed with difficulty, 1934. (Mrs Doris Tilley)

The Honddu River from Watergate. (Malcolm Morrison)

Honddu

The River Honddu rises high on Epynt hills where a multitude of streams converge to form a river. It then runs for around 11 miles in a southerly direction through the pretty Priory Groves to its confluence with the Usk just above Llanfaes bridge. Its history, until recent times, was industrial for most of its passage through Brecon, its waters fuelling industry via a series of weirs, mill races, and reservoirs. All of this hydro-powered industry is now extinct and in the main dismantled, but evidence of its past is all around to remind us of its heritage.

Nowadays the crystal-clear waters offer some very challenging fly fishing. When it floods, the waters take on a deep reddish tint far different in colour to the waters of the Usk, providing an unusual dual colouring where the waters meet just upstream of the Usk Bridge. This strange phenomenon is due to the pigments in the soil in the Epynt hills being very different from those of the Usk valley.

Heol y Ddefaid (aka Ship Street)

The origin of the name has long been a puzzle, but Ship Street, we can be reasonably sure, is a corruption of Sheep Street ('Shepe Street' on John Speed's town plan of 1610). Was this the area where sheep were openly sold on the streets before Brecon had a designated market? The bilingual signage in Ship Street gives the Welsh version as *Heol y Ddefaid*, which translates correctly into the original Welsh name.

There are many interesting and ancient buildings here, all on the southern side. Much of an equally interesting northern side was demolished in a road widening project in the 1950s, but surviving photographs show it in its former charm. The southern side of Ship Street is worth a moment of our time; look at the ornamental woodwork of the gable end of the medieval building (restored in 1963, and again in

2019) near the top of the hill. Alongside it are completely differing styles of nineteenth-century shops and houses creating an odd but interesting street; none conforms to any pattern or style and gives it a uniquely odd skyline. The less said about the modern northern side of the street is, perhaps, the better.

Boleyn House standing halfway along was formerly known as the Swan Inn. It was renamed by its owners, the Williams family of Penpont. Some residents have claimed there is a ghostly presence here, but most former residents deny experiencing anything untoward. One lady did relate that she recalled a duvet being pulled off her bed – an event after which the spirit was told very sternly to leave! Ghostly monks, have been observed from a flat on the corner of Ship Street, walking from the Wheat Street area in the direction the cathedral; the sound of their robes was heard swishing as they went by...

Ship Street near the river, 2016. (Malcolm Morrison)

Ship Street looking down the hill, 2019. (Malcolm Morrison)

Infirmary

The town's Infirmary was once located on the northern side of the Watton, approximately opposite today's Rugby Club. It served the town for many years before the opening of the new War Memorial Hospital in Cerrigcochian Road in 1928. The old infirmary continued to offer a variety of clinics long after the new hospital opened. Recent social media posts have left fond memories of the medical staff who were based there: Mr Sutcliffe, Miss Leaf, and Nurse Parry are remembered with affection. Within the building were the offices of the registrar of births, marriages and deaths, post-natal clinics and various council officials. The clinic was eventually demolished to make way for a relief road.

The official opening ceremony of the new War Memorial Hospital in 1928 was a bittersweet occasion. The new facilities were officially opened by Lord Glanusk, who became the hospital's first casualty. He collapsed and died, having declared the buildings open just moments earlier.

Brecon War Memorial Hospital c. 1948. Note the Girls' Grammar School top left.

Infantry Battle School

A short distance from Brecon at Dering Lines is the Infantry Battle School (IBS), a centre of excellence where infantry officers and section commanders hone their skills. Dering Lines began life as a tented camp during the First World War, but the present camp dates from the 1930s when it was primarily used as an Infantry Training Centre. The Parachute Regiment located here in 1961 and developed the academy that evolved into the Infantry Battle School. Gurkha Company (Mandalay) has been based here for several years and their association with the town is evidenced in the evolving population and certain businesses in the town. Leaders on operations are required to perform extremely difficult and dangerous tasks and the training at the IBS is designed to prepare them to lead their troops to success. Training is intense, covering conventional warfare, counter-insurgency, peacekeeping and supporting roles. The school also provides specialist training teams to assist foreign forces, and allocates some places on courses to overseas students. Courses include:

All Arms NCO Skill at Arms Instructor Course
Basic Tactics Course
Dismounted Close Combat Trainer
Infantry Warrant Officers' Course
Platoon Commanders' Battle Course
Platoon Sergeants' Battle Course
Platoon Tactics Course
SAS Infantry Skills Course
Section Commanders' Battle Course
An alternative and unflattering take on the school calls it bleak, soulless, depressing, windswept and rain-soaked, with nothing but some creaky 'C' Type huts to shield you from the incessant elemental buffeting of Brecon!

The Infantry Battle School, Dering Lines. (Malcolm Morrison)

Jones, Theophilus

Born 18 October 1759 at Brecon, the man who was destined to become the county historian spent much of his boyhood at his grandfather's home in Llangammarch Wells and inherited several historical documents from him. He was educated at Christ College and went on to practise in law, but after being appointed deputy-registrar of the archdeaconry he devoted himself to historical research, living in his father's former house in Lion Street.

Theophilus Jones, county historian.

His major work, *The History of the County of Brecknock*, was written here, the first volume published in 1805; volume two followed in 1809. He had intended writing a history of Radnorshire, but this was never completed. Towards the end of his life we know that he suffered with swollen and bandaged hands and his feet, affected by gout, and must have suffered much pain. He died on 15 January 1812. A second edition of his county history with some additions was published in 1898 in a single volume. A third four-volume edition produced by the county historical society appeared in 1930. This handsome work came with copious additions and is known as the Glanusk Edition.

All That Jazz!

Brecon Jazz Festival has been held annually in August since 1984. Many famous musicians from across the world have graced its stages, and Brecon Jazz is very much on the music calendar. Helen Shapiro, Sonny Rollins, Cleo Laine, Scott Hamilton, Van Morrison, Amy Winehouse, Humphrey Lyttelton, George Melly, Joan Armatrading, Cerys Matthews, Dionne Warwick, Jools Holland, and Courtney Pine are among the visitors. Originally there were many street-corner and open-air stages but more recently the festival seems to have become more focussed in larger venues. An alternative 'Fringe Festival' has developed in the smaller venues throughout the town and adds colour and a fun element to the world-famous main events.

King Street

King Street is a short, narrow, cobbled footpath opposite the Priory Hill junction in the Struet. It is often referred to as King Charles Steps, as the cobbled steps that make up most of its length are a more realistic description; however, the connection to King Charles' overnight stay in Brecon is obscure to say the least. That said, it remains a quaint and interesting place to visit and the climb to the top gives the reward of one of the nicest views of the southerly aspect of the cathedral.

King Goodwill Zwelithini kaBhekuzulu

King Goodwill Zwelithini kaBhekuzulu of the Zulu nation was welcomed to Brecon during his tour of the UK in 2019. The trip included visits to the cathedral and the Royal Welsh Show, but most memorable perhaps was the Cultural and Historical

Zulu King Goodwill at Brecon Barracks, July 2019. (Andrew Williams)

Pageant held at the Barracks on 21 July 2019. Brecon has a close friendship with the Zulu nations' royal family, with many royal visits having taken place over the years.

Kensington

Kensington is a small residential area bordering the entrance to the Promenade. It seems it was fashionable at one time to name streets after famous areas of London. Its chapel is its only building worthy of mention. There are several quaint and pretty little side streets nearby including Kensington Row and Mill Street that are worth a visit.

Llanfaes

Llanfaes is a parish to the east of the Usk Bridge. Its name translates roughly as 'church in the meadow' and, in the main, it is an extremely nice area to live. Llanfaes is the lowest and flattest part of Brecon and in the early part of the nineteenth century, due mainly to poor sanitation, it had the lowest life expectancy of all of Brecon's districts. Here was the most disease and the greatest proportion of deaths. Mortality in 1841 in Llanfaes was 3.3 per cent whereas the average for the whole town was 2.3 per cent, which itself was considered high for a town without a large manufacturing base.

Llanfaes begins in Bridge Street, one side being residential, the other part of the Christ College campus. Orchard Street follows where there once was a public house known as The Coach and Horses. It gave up its licence in the 1940s and, as its name implies, was once one of the town's many coaching inns. It was reputed to have once had a rather nasty ghost. Several years ago, the owners slept in a room on the ground floor that had once been used to store barrels of beer. Here they encountered the spirit that appeared moments after the lady of the house went to bed for the night. As

Part of Bridge Street/Orchard Street in Llanfaes. (Malcolm Morrison)

she was about to get into bed, a man dressed in a dark cloak and hood got out of bed on the other side and walked right through the wall. She called for her husband and he remembers that the room felt deadly cold, and had a peculiar smell, the like of which he hasn't encountered before or since. On a different occasion the wife saw the ghost again and this time it went straight through the window. They are reputed to be a very down-to-earth couple and not given to fantasies. Fear not however; the spirit hasn't reappeared since – to my knowledge!

Lion Street

Lion Street was originally one of the prime streets of Brecon in what was known as Cantercilly Ward. The area today is quite narrow and is not the desirable residential district of old. It contains many very old and interesting buildings and one of Brecon's most pretty chapels (The Plough), but the area is mainly commercial with supermarkets and a retail precinct replacing Dr Cokes and Bethel chapels. Roughly halfway along its length stand a number of ancient buildings that include Bishop Bevan Hall. Much of the building to the west of the entrance passage once made up Church House Men's Club, once a very popular social meeting place where the menfolk of Brecon spent their leisure time. Much of the building is early seventeenth century and is well worth a few moments of our time; however, the once popular Men's Club is no more but is remembered with affection by many who mis-spent their youth and manhood there.

Lion Yard

Lion Yard was formerly the yard and stabling of the Golden Lion Inn that occupied most of this area and today's Bethel Square. It is now a pretty commercial area with some interesting shops and a lovely tourist information centre located between the town's major car park and Lion Street.

Lion Yard, Brecon, 2019.
(Malcolm Morrison)

Llanddew

Near the hamlet of Llanddew on the outskirts of Brecon is a farm named Sandel. A map of the area made in the nineteenth century records that 'Local tradition has it that Henry VII planted his standard at this place on his march from Pembroke to Shrewsbury.' This is certainly not true as Henry Tudor's route to Bosworth Field is well known and did not pass this way; however, an army under Rhys ap Thomas, a nobleman from Carmarthen, stopped here on route to join Henry's forces in 1485, and it is very likely that it was he who raised Henry Tudor's standard on his march from Carmarthen via Brecon to Welshpool to join the Tudor cause. Rhys had been tasked with intercepting and harassing Henry Tudor's army along their march to oppose the king. Rhys instead gathered support as he travelled through Brecon to join Henry's army. It is recorded that Rhys's intervention was crucial in Henry's success.

Rhys is sometimes credited with delivering the mortal blow to end Richard III's reign. A chronicler recorded that a Welshman struck the death blow with a halberd while Richard's horse was stuck in the marshy ground. It was said the blows were so violent that the king's helmet was driven into his skull. Perhaps there is a Brecon connection in the turn of events at Bosworth Field.

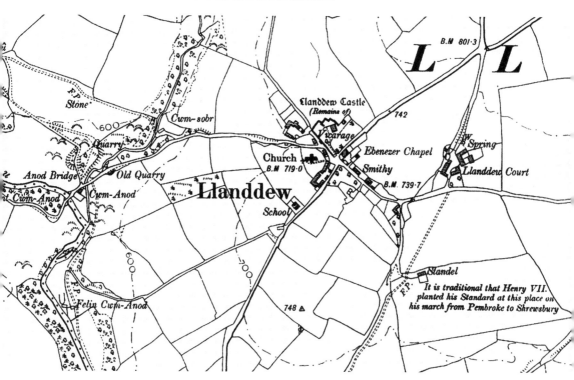

Llandew village and the rallying point for the march to Bosworth Field.

Colourful houses on St Michael's Street, 2019. (Malcolm Morrison)

Lôn y Popty

Lôn y Popty is the seventeenth-century name for today's St Michael's Street. It has been suggested that the name translates as 'Bakery Lane'. In 1819 the street was called Three Cocks Lane, suggesting a nearby inn, and following the building of St Michael's Church in 1851, the modern name of St Michael's Street was adopted.

It is a quaint location with some lovely views across the river towards the beacons. A house along its way has a quite amusing plate mounted upon its wall which is worth looking out for.

Limekilns

A short distance beyond Tollgate Bridge on the Brecon Canal, keeping to the road that runs next to the towpath, just beyond the rugby ground is a series of strange stone arches just beneath the canal bank. These are limestone kilns, a relic of Victorian industry. Limestone was transported here in huge quantities via the canal and broken up, mixed with coal and burned to produce lime for agricultural purposes. It is said that homeless people often slept on top of the kilns during cold weather in order to keep warm; however, sometimes the wind direction changed, and it was not unknown for an unfortunate sleeper to become asphyxiated by fumes from the kilns. Unsubstantiated stories suggest that the bodies were sometimes disposed of by being thrown into the kilns and cremated. Brecon's limekilns are currently being restored.

Mount Street

The name Mount Street seems to have mutated from Mouse Street, as it is given on early town plans (Rheol Lygoden in the Welsh language). The street layout has changed a little following road improvement over the years and perhaps its most interesting feature, apart from its name, is the school that lies along its way.

Market Street

Market Street, once known as Horn Lane, runs from Watergate along the banks of the Honddu River until it links with Heol Gouesnou at its junction with Market Street. It was once residential and commercial but most of the buildings along its length have been demolished, widening and improving the area, although some commercial enterprises remain.

Market Street (rear of market hall). (Malcolm Morrison)

The iconic stained glass at St Mary's, 2018. (Malcolm Morrison)

St Mary's Church

Although technically a chapel of ease for the Priory church, in 1802 St Mary's was the fashionable church in Brecon, boasting an organ and organist. The iconic tower was built by the ill-fated Duke of Buckingham. His rise to greatness and subsequent fall from grace and execution at Tower Hill on 17 May 1521 have been covered elsewhere.

Maen Du

Maen Du, the best known of Brecon's Holy Wells, lies in quiet woodland just north of the town. It resembles an early Christian monastic cell from which its waters rise. Maen du indicates a black or dark stone; its waters run along a channel into a stone-lined pool which may once have been used for bathing in the holy waters. The tradition is that

The Maen Ddu Holy Well. (Malcolm Morrison)

it's a wishing well for lovelorn maidens and lovers who believed the water would make their wishes come true. It is well worth a visit, accessed by a footpath from the nearby housing estate. Personally, I wouldn't recommend drinking the waters from this or, for that matter, any of the other Holy Wells nearby; maybe throw a small coin in or anoint yourself with the water and make a wish ... you never know!

Maybery, Richard

Richard Maybery, the First World War flying ace, was born in Brecon in 1895, an only son. He graduated from Sandhurst and served for several years in the army in India until he was seriously wounded in action. Following recovery in the UK, he took up flying and became an expert in low-flight attack. In April 1917, he was with 56 Squadron in France where his bravery was honoured. He was awarded the Military Cross 'For conspicuous gallantry and devotion to duty', for attacking aerodromes at low altitudes, mounted men and a goods train. He next attacked and shot down a hostile aircraft and, before returning, attacked a passenger train.

A bar was added to his Military Cross on 17 December 1917 'For conspicuous gallantry and devotion to duty as leader of offensive patrols for three months, during which he personally destroyed nine enemy aeroplanes and drove down three out of control. On one occasion, having lost his patrol, he attacked a formation of eight enemy aeroplanes. One was seen to crash, and two others went down, out of control, the formation being completely broken up.' Maybery was too brave to survive the war. On 19 December 1917, two days after winning his second Military Cross, he shot down his twenty-first enemy plane but was hit by anti-aircraft fire and killed, aged just twenty-two.

First World War flying ace Richard Maybery.

Morgan, Gwenllian

Gwenllian Morgan was born on 9 April 1852, a century or more before the term feminist became commonly used. The daughter of a curate, Miss Philip Morgan (as she preferred to be known) took an avid interest in local history and became prominent in public life. She was first elected to Brecon Town Council in 1907 but perhaps is best remembered for becoming Brecon, and Wales', first lady mayor in the year 1910. During her year in office she had to overcome bigotry, misogyny and prejudice from some of her peers but, although she may have been upset by this, it certainly didn't deter her – at the time, Westminster and the right to vote were still completely barred to women.

   Her popularity is evident from the results of the 1920 council election. She came an easy second in the ballot, polling 1,088 votes and comfortably retaining her seat. She continued to serve the Borough of Brecon for many years afterwards. A supporter of the temperance movement, she became president of the Brecon branch, serving on the Board of Guardians with Adelaide Williams, another woman ahead of her time. Her interest in the early life of Henry Vaughan led to work on an edition of the poet's work, but the project was never completed. Her work though did form the basis for a later book about the celebrated poet. The University of Wales conferred an Honorary MA degree upon her in 1925. She died in Brecon on 7 November 1939. Gwenllian Morgan Court is named in her honour. She was probably Brecon's first feminist.

Gwenllian Morgan Court, 2019. (Malcolm Morrison)

Newgate Street

Newgate Street is the last street in Llanfaes, and it was here, on the banks of the Tarell River, that the County Gaol stood. Its bloody past is covered elsewhere but the building has been demolished and replaced with housing whose façade is based upon the original gaol's design. The only other interesting features hereabouts are the Gwtws footpath, the Brecon Golf Club and the beautiful Elizabethan farmhouse of Newton Farm, and the ancient watering hole the Drovers Arms.

A lady who lived at the Drovers witnessed several unexplained happenings whilst there. Both she and her husband heard someone walking along a corridor into a bedroom which was found to be empty. They once spent a night in that room and

Newgate Street from the Drovers Arms, 2019. (Malcolm Morrison)

saw the apparition of a man in a tall hat, which totally freaked them out. Another lady stated that the house next door to the Drovers had a horrible man ghost that 'used to play hell with her' when she lived there in 1985.

Nythfa

Nythfa is a large mansion house located in woodland in the Struet area but is accessed from the Belle Vue road. Currently it is a holiday hotel, but the building has gone through several changes of use over the years. People who worked there remember meeting a grey lady on the main stairs, and also the figure of a little boy near the kitchen. Another lady arriving for a night shift regularly saw a figure in a window facing the drive, which she mistook for a resident; eventually she realised it wasn't. No recent sightings have been reported.

de Neufmarché, Bernard

Norman armies led by Bernard de Neufmarché swept across these lands, subjugating all and establishing their castle at the junction of the Usk and Honddu rivers around the year 1093. It was around this castle that the town we now know as Brecon grew and flourished. Neufmarché is remembered by the anglicised Newmarch Street in Llanfaes; Rhyd-Bernard (Bernard's ford), an ancient fording place on the River Usk; and Rhyd-Bernard Terrace, a short row near Mill Street. Brecon seems to have few direct references to their former Normans lords. The priory that became our cathedral was also begun by Neufmarché. It was originally a Benedictine priory dedicated to St John the Evangelist.

Old Gaol

The Old Gaol, as Brecon County Gaol was known, stood on the banks of the River Tarell in Llanfaes. It dated from 1778, replacing an infamous prison in the Watton. Male prisoners sentenced to hard labour were employed on a treadmill; women were

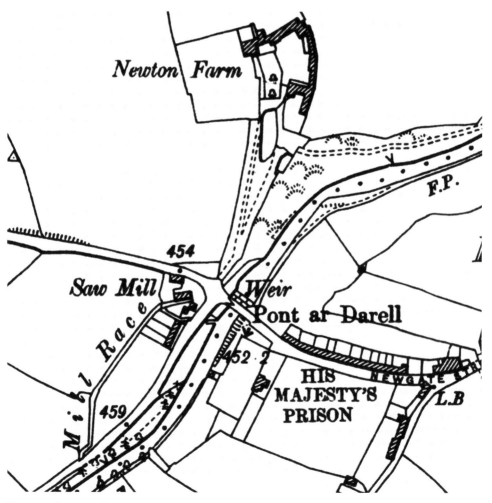

Newgate Street *c.* 1890.

employed washing, mending, cleaning and knitting. A 'silent system' was the rule for convicted prisoners.

Here are some crimes recorded. Nineteen-year-old Joseph Robinson was sentenced to death for burglary in 1817. In April 1845, a crowd estimated to be in excess of 15,000 or more crowded along the western banks of the river to witness the execution of Thomas Thomas on the gaol side. The executioner was incompetent, and the condemned man took several minutes to die. Again, in 1861, an execution was botched by the same hangman and nineteen-year-old William Williams suffered a slow and agonising death, so much so that the crowd howled abuse at the hangman and a constable who tried to intervene. In 1895, a seventeen-year-old was sentenced to three months' hard labour for stealing two casks of ale.

The gaol was reconstructed in 1858 and was eventually replaced by the residential flats and renamed Cwrt Tarell in 1975.

Orchard Street

Orchard Street is a road in Llanfaes located between Bridge and Church streets. There is no actual orchard remaining here in modern times, however the very last house in the street is called Orchard House and houses in its grounds are named Orchard Gardens. The area today is part of the Christ College campus, but the names offer some evidence of the former function of this area – perhaps an orchard associated with the Friary or even the castle?

Old Port Superior

Old Port Superior is an area marked on John Speed's plan of the town dated 1610. It appears to be the area we now call Priory Hill. Port is an Old English word for gateway or place where travellers or goods may enter or leave under supervision. The use of Superior seems to indicate the proximity to the castle. The old map doesn't appear to show any road in the area we now know as the Postern, but the 'port' seems to be in the general area where today's entrance to the cathedral Chapter House stands. In later years Old Port Superior was a Ward of the town covering the Priory area.

Old Port Inferior

Old Port Inferior is indicated on the same map as above at a location midway along today's Struet. Once again it may relate to the place where incoming goods or people are met and checked. In later years Old Port Inferior was a Ward of the town covering the Struet area.

P

Pen-y-crug

Pen-y-crug, the large hill that overlooks the town, is probably the most impressive example of an Iron Age hill fort in the district. It is easily accessed from midway along the road between Cradoc village and the B4520 road to Upper Chapel where there is a convenient lay-by to park. The views from on top are truly spectacular, as are the remains of the ditches and earthworks that have survived the millennia. A reasonably good footpath takes one right to the summit. It is a fairly easy climb and taking a camera is recommended.

Brecon Beacons from Pen-y-crug Iron Age hill fort, 2019. (Malcolm Morrison)

The Priory Groves, 2018. (Malcolm Morrison)

Priory Groves

Priory Groves is a quiet and beautiful woodland walk leading from the cathedral along the bank of the River Honddu. One footpath runs close to the riverbank, passing a hidden cave along its route, and eventually merging with the path that runs along the higher ground. Near the Priory entrance is a freshwater spring emerging from a stone wall with stone steps leading down to it. This is the ancient and holy Priory Well, where dropping pins or coins into its waters was reputed to allow the granting of a wish.

The well originally served the Priory and its waters famously continued to flow through severe summer droughts and were never known to freeze in winter. Its flow today is diminished from years past, possibly due to extensive construction work on the fields nearby, which may have affected the local hydrology. The waters were once collected further down the hill in a small reservoir, which is thought by some to have been the source of Brecon's first piped water supply. Excavations many years ago in the Struet uncovered wooden pipes which appear to have carried the supply to the Bulwark.

The meandering paths through the Groves have several entries and exit points, giving choices to walkers who can journey as far as Llanddew should they wish. Look out for the small hidden cave.

Promenade

The Promenade was built to attract visitors to Brecon, opening in 1894. The Prom, as it is affectionately known, is a peaceful walk following the banks of the Usk along a footpath that commences at the Honddu Bridge. It passes the canal intake, the 'Men's Pool' and the former bandstand with some spectacular views until one reaches the boathouse and café. By the middle of the twentieth century, miners and factory workers from the South Wales valleys flocked here with their families in halcyon summers past. Here they could hire a rowing boat or a pedalo, enjoy a picnic lunch on the riverbank, buy an ice cream, play games with their families on the riverbank or simply enjoy the scenic views across Newton Park towards the Brecon Beacons.

The most popular location for swimming was the 'Men's Pool' just below the promenade boathouse with changing rooms and a viewing gallery above. Swimming here is rare nowadays as the town has an indoor pool but, in its day, 'the Promenade Swimming Club' (a concept rather than an actual entity) was where the majority of Breconians learned to swim. It was a kind of 'badge of courage' for novices to make their first crossing of the river here. Many a novice swimmer 'chickened out' halfway across and turned back before eventually making a successful crossing, resting for a few euphoric moments before making the return crossing. The waters run over a weir here and are slow moving and reasonably safe, and I haven't come across any stories of major mishaps here.

The Promenade Boathouse, 2012. (Malcolm Morrison)

The 'Men's Pool' and Bandstand, from Brecon Show, Newton Park. (Wynne Rees)

It remains an extremely popular feature with both young and old alike; however swimming in the river has become a rarity, and the bandstand in the background of the photo a thing of the past.

Postern

The Postern is an area close to the ruins of the castle which runs in a north-easterly direction bordering the banks of the Honddu towards Priory Hill. A postern gate was historically a small gateway or entrance in a castle wall but the actual location of this one is lost in time. Postern gates were often concealed to allow the occupants to come and go unseen.

This short but interesting street retains the name long after the disappearance of its gate. Along its length we find one of the town's early prisons (in private ownership) and remnants of the huge railway viaduct and the archway that once led to a goods yard that stood here. A flight of rough steps runs down to the riverbank from a point just beyond the bridge. Here, hidden in overgrown briars, are the remains of a substantial but dry well-inscribed 'Sir Charles Morgan Bart'. This is recorded on early maps as 'Burvas Well'.

The Postern Gaol was built in 1842. It contained a courtroom and housed the police station and cells where felons and debtors were held, serving the community for thirty-two years. Debtors fared badly and cells were set aside for those who exceeded their means. At Christmas 1844, Howell Gwyn Esq. High Sherriff of the county, kindly treated all the debtor prisoners to a substantial dinner of roast beef and plum pudding on Christmas Day, and Thomas Batt, Esq., surgeon to the gaol, presented them with a quantity of prime beef. Mr Harry Simmons, who currently owns the Postern Gaol building, has a few interesting yarns about the gaol life and may be around to relate them to you.

Below left: The Postern showing remains of viaduct. (Malcolm Morrison)

Below right: The Burvas Well, The Postern. (Malcolm Morrison)

Queen's Head

The Queen's Head was once a popular hotel in Market Street. It was the meeting place of the Royal Antediluvian Order of Buffaloes (RAOB), one of the largest fraternal organisations that became extremely popular in the nineteenth century. It was similar in many ways to Freemasonry, but membership was open to all males over eighteen who declared they were true and loyal supporters of the British Crown and Constitution. The organization is still alive and well, but I don't believe the once popular Brecon Lodge is effective any longer.

The Queen's Head closed and was demolished during the latter part of the twentieth century. All that remains today is a car-parking area where it once stood near the Castle Street/Market Street junction.

The Royal Antediluvian Order of Buffaloes at the Queen's Head, Market Street.

Queen Elizabeth II

Queen Elizabeth II's first visit to Brecon coincided with the bicentenary of the Brecknock Agricultural Society in August 1955. It was a lovely bright day and the young queen arrived at the railway station in Camden Road to be met by General Raikes and a deputation from the town. Huge crowds turned out to welcome her, lining the streets along her route.

She spent the day at the showground at Newton Park, taking great interest in the exhibits, especially the cattle and native Welsh ponies. The great and the good of the county were invited to dine with Her Majesty on the showground. Her Majesty revisited on 27 July 1983 to attend a service at Brecon Cathedral to celebrate the Diamond Jubilee of the Diocese of Swansea and Brecon.

Welsh Cob taking a bite of the Queen's posy, Brecon Show, 1955.

Rugby

Brecon RFC were founder members of the Welsh Rugby Football Union and the first recorded match played by a Brecon team can be traced back to 1868. The club celebrated its centenary during the 1979/80 seasons. Another of the club's claims to fame is that local boy Richard Davies Garnons Williams, a former player, represented Wales at forward in their first ever international match against England in February 1881. Richard came from a very old Breconshire family and although a serving army officer, he still continued to play for Newport RFC and occasionally for Brecon.

Wales were reduced to thirteen players by half-time, but Richard stuck manfully to his task as the Welsh pack struggled to compete. Some reports claim Wales finished with only eleven fit men, but history was made on that day for Wales and Brecon RFC.

Aged fifty-eight at the outbreak of the First World War, Williams rejoined the army and served with distinction until he was killed in action in 1915. One of his men wrote, 'He was with us all the time in the front trench, we could not have had a better, braver officer.' He was fifty-nine at the time of his death, the oldest Welsh rugby international to die in the war.

Brecon's Richard Garnons Williams represented Wales in the first England-Wales international.

The Watton from
Brecon Rugby
Club, 2019.
(Malcolm Morrison)

Perhaps the 2018/19 season will go down in Brecon Rugby Club's history as one of their most successful. Brecon won a magnificent late victory in the Welsh RFU National Plate at the Principality Stadium in Cardiff, defeating Bonymaen RFC 21-23. The next day the town turned out in huge numbers to watch a unique procession, not in the usual open-top bus but a tractor and trailer to reflect Brecon's agricultural heritage. There was still work to be done to achieve a league and cup double and, two days later, the team secured the league win they needed to guarantee that they would be crowned as Champions of Division 1 East. A remarkable double.

Railways

The Neath and Brecon railway reached Brecon in 1867 with a temporary station at Mount Street. At this time, Brecon had two other railway stations: the Brecon to Merthyr line at the Watton station and the Mid-Wales railway using Free Street station. Obviously three stations were not viable and 'Free Street Joint station' served all lines from 1871. The station was actually in today's Camden Road, a seemingly unnamed road at the time. Almost all of the railway through Brecon was elevated, as early photographs show.

Just how much the railways changed the lives of Brecon people is apparent when in 1904 the greatest show ever to visit our fair county rolled into Builth Wells, a nearby town to the north of Brecon. William F. Cody (Buffalo Bill) and his touring show (or exhibition, as he preferred to call it) made its one and only visit to Powys during the last ever tour of Europe. The show had excited and enthralled kings and queens and the great and the good throughout Europe, focusing on the story of the Wild West and, of course, Buffalo Bill's part in it.

Three trains carrying the massive ensemble arrived at 4 a.m. to be met by a huge and excited crowd. There followed a procession from the station to the show site led by Buffalo Bill himself with his entourage of hundreds, which included many native American Indians. Two sell-out performances were given, at 2 p.m. and 7 p.m., the

Above: Brecon railway station *c.* 1890.

Below: Brecon *c.* 1940. Note the elevated railway. (Adele Evans and Noreen Richards)

last finishing at 10 p.m. Special trains were laid on for the two shows, packed tightly with excited people from all over the district with a good number from Brecon making the journey.

A young lad recorded at the time: 'During our school holidays, we saw on the hoarding's brilliant posters advertising Buffalo Bill's Wild West. What a splendid figure Buffalo Bill made with his long hair, black sombrero, goatee beard and silver spurs, mounted on a beautiful white horse, twirling his revolver around his finger; and there were real Indians, too!' Alas, the poor lad was not taken to see the show.

Amazingly the whole show was dismantled, packed and en route to its next venue by 11 p.m. The photographs on this page show fragments of the actual poster hoardings used at the show that were discovered after being lost for 110 years.

The railway lines to all the local stations in the Brecon area closed in 1964.

Brecon railway station in Camden Road *c.* 1960.

Large fragments of the Buffalo Bill hoardings discovered in 2017. (Malcolm Morrison)

The Struet

The origins of this name are obscure. Some believe it is a misspelling of Street. Hugh Thomas (1698) describes the ward Old Port Inferior as all the lands on the banks of the Honddu from the 'Strowed Gate' northwards to the parish of Llanthew ... 'a fair broad street from the town gate to the Priory bridge and is called the Strowed'. The Welsh word 'Struwedd', I believe, translates as structures. Yet another offering is that the name derives from the Welsh 'yr Ystrywaid', which is believed to have been the fifteenth-century name for the region which includes the cathedral. It is easy to see how the Welsh 'y' or 'yr' could have mutated into 'the'.

A large building at the Struet/Mount Street junction was once a specialist bookshop selling historical and antiquarian books run by Mr Gwyn Evans, a very knowledgeable and respected gentleman affectionately known as Gwyn the Books. He recalled seeing a ghost in his shop on more than one occasion. The harmless spirit, a lady,

The Struet from Heol Gouesnou/Mount Street junction, 2019. (Malcolm Morrison)

The Struet from George Street junction, 2019. (Malcolm Morrison)

walked through the solid walls of the building towards the premises next door, a photographer's shop at the time.

The George Hotel is a late seventeenth-century coaching inn with many interesting features and at least one reported ghostly happening. A group of young ladies enjoying lunch one day in 2009 experienced an alarming occurrence. Suddenly and without warning the glasses on their table began to slowly move – and not all in the same direction. The event lasted less than one minute but the young ladies quickly left.

Sarah Siddons

The actress Sarah Siddons was born here in Brecon on 5 July 1755. A touring group of the eighteenth century called 'The Strolling Players' paid frequent visits to Brecon, but had it not been for the birth of the greatest actresses of her era at an inn in the main street of our town, it is doubtful whether they would have been remembered at all. Sarah was the daughter of the actor-manager Roger Kemble, a man who travelled the country with his small troop entertaining people in country inns and market squares. Records of the birth of Sarah Kemble at the 'Shoulder of Mutton' in the High Street and her baptism on 14 July of the same year gives her parents as 'Strolling Players'. Roger Kemble, her father, was a regular visitor to Brecon. We know he returned in April 1758 and again in 1770. His last recorded visit was in 1775.

Tradition has it that actor William Siddons, a member of Kemble's troop, proposed to Sarah during a performance at The Bell Inn at Brecon. If this were true, then it would probably have happened during the 1775 visit when Sarah would have been aged twenty. The announcement caused dismay to her parents, who had intended her to marry someone of 'greater quality' and Sarah was sent off to work as a maid. Her parents eventually relented, and she returned to the company and married Siddons. They had children, but the marriage was not a success and ended in separation.

Sarah Siddons became the most renowned actress of eighteenth-century Britain, but she did not impress on her first appearance at Drury Lane and her services were

The Sarah Siddons, formerly the Shoulder of Mutton Inn, 2019. (Malcolm Morrison)

not further required. She spent six years touring the provinces but returned to the London theatre in 1782 and became an instant success.

Over the next twenty years she became the toast of Drury Lane and Covent Garden. Her beauty and stunning looks made her an ideal choice for lead roles. She easily and effortlessly showed the passion required for her favourite role, Lady Macbeth, said to be so powerful that audiences swooned and often had to be helped out of the theatre in various stages of distress. And yet she was born in our little town of Brecon in a small room above the tavern then called The Shoulder of Mutton Inn. Presently the inn is known as The Sarah Siddons; the inn sign displays a portrait of her.

Slang

Brecon is unique in many ways, but I'm sometimes surprised to hear certain words that appear peculiar to the district. These words were commonly used back in the 1950s and '60s and quite possibly predate this – I may be mistaken but I have never heard them spoken anywhere else.

The first are terms of endearment, used in similar circumstances with roughly the same meaning as 'pal' or 'mate', but most certainly are not disrespectful.
Surrey/Sloper – I was quite surprised to hear this after a gap of over sixty years. 'How's it going, Sloper,' or 'Okay Surrey?' *Gouga* – once again, 'How's it going, Gouga?', sometimes shortened to 'Alright Gouge?'

Another is the rough-sounding word *Sklem*. To sklem something is to blag or obtain it for nothing, but is regarded as acceptable, even held in regard, unlike scrounging or cadging, which are looked upon as annoying. If someone is extremely adept at skleming something they could be referred to as a 'chief sklemer'.

I'm sure most Breconians are familiar with '*Bombies*', a strange little fish that hides under stones in our rivers. Their correct name is Bullheads, and I believe they lay their eggs under the stones and the male fish guard them; however, in Brecon they will forever be bombies.

Another strange resident in our rivers is the caddis fly larva, found under stones living inside a protective tube of minute pebbles where they mature. They were called 'Corbetts' when I was young and were a favourite (and possibly illegal) bait for trout fishing.

Saint Mary's Street

Saint Mary's Street runs from the Bulwark towards Wheat Street. There are few interesting buildings along its length but there are some very nice specialist shops and businesses. The town's post office was once located here as well as the GP surgery. The entrance into St Mary's from this side has an interesting dog-door, reputedly used to eject troublesome dogs during religious services by way of a pair of iron tongs! Today the dog-door is just a façade.

Saint Mary's Street, 2019.
(Malcolm Morrison)

Steeple Lane from
the Bulwark, 2019.
(Malcolm Morrison)

Steeple Lane

Steeple Lane is a short lane that runs around the Buckingham Tower linking High Street with Church Lane and Saint Mary's Street. Its name seems slightly odd as the church has a tower and not a steeple. The only explanation I can offer is that perhaps the name survives from an earlier steeple on the church (which was originally a chapel of ease for the priory) before the building of the Buckingham Tower.

Street Names

Brecon's medieval street names are predominantly English in origin. It was fashionable years ago to name streets after English places and towns as in Kensington and London Row. In fact, Welsh street names are bit of a rarity, and where they do exist, they are usually mis-pronounced, for example Ffynnon Dewi is often called Funnun Jewee; or Pendre – the slightly less annoying Pendray. These days pronunciation has improved, probably due to better education. Many of our streets are named after prominent inns, for example Lion Street, or specific buildings as in Chapel Street. Often the names have outlived the features they commemorate.

Schooling in the Nineteenth Century

A plan to create Brecon Benevolent Schools was hatched in 1809, its aim being to teach the children of the poor 'the three Rs' and acquire knowledge of religion. Archdeacon Richard Davies (of whom we read earlier) became president of the schools that he worked hard to establish. Money was raised for building schoolrooms and to support the boys' and girls' schools. Two existing charity schools were merged into the new institutions that opened in February 1811. Four years later it was clear that the schools were a great success; the boys' school had admitted 172 scholars, and the girls (whose curriculum included needlework) 163.

The school day ran from 9 a.m. to 2 p.m. and considerable attention was given to religious teaching, pupils being required to attend morning service at St Mary's. Much emphasis was given to personal cleanliness: pupils with dirty hands and faces were made to wash in front of children of the opposite gender as a means of shaming them. Obstinate offenders were also punished in front of their peers of the opposite gender; this punishment was probably not corporal punishment as Archdeacon Davies claimed that the system was one of reward, and the only punishment was that of shame. He claimed he had not detected a single falsehood in either school for over two years. He contributed towards building costs and made an annual subscription of ten guineas towards the upkeep. Boys seeking apprenticeships were given four or five guineas to enable them to obtain their goal.

In 2019 a new secondary school at Penlan is nearing completion. It will replace the comprehensive school built during the 1960s.

Above: Brecon High School (formerly Brecon Secondary Modern), 2019. (Malcolm Morrison)

Below: Former Brecon Boys' Grammar School (now Brecon High School), 2019. (Malcolm Morrison)

Tarell

Brecon's three rivers are designated as a special area of conservation, containing some rare species including the otter and a variety of fish and birds. The Tarell originates near Storey Arms in the valley below the area historically known as Cadair Arthur (today the peaks of Pen y Fan and Corn Ddu). The name Tarell seems to have defied explanation, but the pretty river runs for 12 miles in a north-westerly direction to join the Usk just below the promenade boathouse. Although it runs for a short distance through Brecon's industrial park, it is in the main a pretty, clear and gentle unpolluted river, with good trout fishing for much of its length. But don't be deceived

River Tarell near Newton Green.
(Malcolm Morrison)

by its gentle serene manner. When heavy rains fall it can quickly become a raging torrent, flooding Silver Street and Newton Green in days past.

Town Walls

Brecon was once a walled town, quite like Conwy, but today only fragments remain following their destruction soon after the Civil War. Fragments of the walls, some earthworks and the remains of a tower and gatehouse are protected as scheduled monuments. Some believe that the towns burgesses demolished its defences to prevent a siege and destruction by the approaching Parliamentary army. There are also traditions that the demolition was carried out by Cromwell's men in 1648. Brecon is known to have aided and supported Charles I, who was welcomed here in 1645, staying at Priory House as the guest of the governor of the town and castle. The king, accompanied by Lifeguards and a large contingent of foot soldiers, stayed overnight and was well entertained. He left Brecon the following morning, local people having supplied enough horses for his foot soldiers to become mounted dragoons. These Royalist sympathies, so clearly displayed during his visit, could explain the stories that Cromwell himself battered and pulled down our castle. Whether it was Cromwell's men or locals that tore down the town walls we shall never know for certain, but the remains of the portions of the ancient walls that have somehow survived lie to the rear of Lion Street bordering the town's car parks, and behind Watton Mount and in the Captains Walk area. Theophilus Jones repeats the popular tradition that Cromwell's men 'battered and pulled down Brecknock Castle' and mentions a manuscript in the British Museum from an officer with the Royalist army, stating that the townspeople destroyed their own defences. We can only guess which version is correct, but the Parliamentary army is known to have spent some time here in 1648 and did much damage in the Priory, and probably elsewhere. At least some portions remain for us to enjoy.

Below left: Remains of old town wall in Brecon car park. (Malcolm Morrison)

Below right: Remains of old town wall in Captains Walk. (Malcolm Morrison)

Usk

The River Usk rises on the northern slopes of the Black Mountain in the Brecon Beacons. Initially it flows north into the Usk reservoir, then around 12 miles eastwards to Brecon, then on to discharge into the Bristol Channel in the Newport wetlands. The Usk and its tributaries are designated as a special area of conservation.

There is just one bridge crossing the Usk in Brecon town, linking Bridge Street with Watergate. The origins of earliest bridges over the river are uncertain but the river was fordable at Rhyd-Bernard, a short distance upstream from the present bridge. The existing stone bridge was built in 1563 to replace an earlier bridge washed away in floods of 1535. It was widened in 1794 but in the 1950s it required further work to accommodate modern road traffic. A new concrete bed with the addition of metal-framed footpaths on either side was placed on top of the original stone base.

River Usk and Promenade. (Malcolm Morrison)

The Usk Bridge from downstream, 2019. (Malcolm Morrison)

I have previously described the result as 'functional and safe but extremely ugly', but nevertheless, it gained Grade I listing in 1976.

U3A – University of the Third Age

U3A reached Britain in 1982. Brecon U3A was founded in 1984 and currently has around 300 members. It is a lifelong learning co-operative for older people no longer in full-time work, providing opportunities to share learning experiences in a range of subjects and groups, not for qualifications but for fun.

Brecon U3A meets most Thursdays in Theatr Brycheiniog; the morning consists of talks on a variety of subjects given by visiting speakers or U3A members. The two afternoon sessions are run by special interest groups, which are too numerous to list in full but include Archaeology, Architecture, Art, Bridge, Theology, Creative Writing, Earth Science, Family History, Gardening, Poetry, and Wildlife to name a few. Some groups meet in other venues on other days for trips, courses and workshops.

Victoria Cross

Very few holders of Britain's most prestigious military honour are buried in Wales, but one of the 'Few', Major Charles Lumley VC, lies almost forgotten in the grounds of Brecon Cathedral. His gallantry and heroism led to him being decorated at the first Victoria Cross investiture on 26 June 1857 by Queen Victoria herself at Hyde Park in London.

Lt Charles Lumley, aged twenty-five, bravely led his men through heavy Russian fire during an attack in the Crimean War, distinguishing himself by his courage and persistence during the assault. During the attack he received terrible wounds to the face and mouth, which horribly disfigured him.

The grave of Major Charles Lumley VC, Brecon Cathedral yard. (Malcolm Morrison)

On the morning of Sunday 17 October 1858, he was found dead at Brecon Barracks. He survived the terrible carnage of Sebastopol but combat stress, and the terrible disfigurement he had suffered in the service of his country, led him to take his own life. His grave is relatively easy to find in the yard almost directly opposite the cathedral entrance. Spend a few moments at his graveside to remember a real hero.

Vaughan, Henry

Henry Vaughan (1621–95) is one of Wales' best-known poets, born near Brecon, where he lived most of his life. He was educated at Jesus College but took no degree. Two years later his father sent him to London to study law. At the outbreak of the Civil War he returned to Wales and entered military service on the Royalist side. He loved the peace of the Usk valley and later he practised medicine here. He was twice married, first to Catherine Wise, and later to her sister Elizabeth. Vaughan was bilingual, and there is a subtle Welsh influence in his poetry, which also reflects his love of his native valley. Between 1646 and 1655 he published several volumes of his poetry including his major work, *Silex Scintillans*, published in two parts in 1650 and 1655.

He died on 23 April 1695 and is buried at Llansantffraid, on the banks of the River Usk. His work influenced William Wordsworth, and the Sassoon Society regularly

Notice board at St Ffraid's Church, Llansaintffraid.

visit the Silurist's final resting place to lay a wreath. Sassoon wrote the tribute poem 'At the grave of Henry Vaughan' in honour of the Silurist. Here are a few lines from the great Henry Vaughan:

> *I saw Eternity the other night*
> *Like a great ring of pure and endless light,*
> *All calm as it was bright.*
> *from 'The World'*

> *My soul, there is a country far beyond the stars*
> *Where stands a winge̩d sentry, all skilful in the wars:*
> *There, above noise and danger, sweet Peace is crowned with smiles,*
> *And One born in a manger commands the beauteous files.*

> *Peace – Silex Scintillans, 1650–05*

The grave of Henry Vaughan, St Ffraid's Church, Llansaintffraid, 2019. (Malcolm Morrison)

W

Water Supply

The town's first water supply according to Edwin Poole began as early as 1587. The water supply fed a 'townys pond' in Glamorgan Street on the South side of St Mary's Church. We believe the source was the same as the supply that was installed around 1776. A Mr Grazebrook laid down wooden pipes in the principal streets of the town and brought the first 'organised supply of water for the use of the town'. The waterworks was situated in a deep dingle at the back of the old brewery in the Struet. The waterworks drew from the Honddu, and very likely from the overspill from the Priory well. The pipes were constructed of wood; in the late nineteenth century some of this piping was uncovered during excavations in the Struet. The wooden pipes were reported as being in reasonably good condition despite the years underground and were 10–12 feet in length, quite large with a 4-inch hole bored in them.

The current waterworks at Bailihelig was completed in 1867. The pipes were of cast iron and the water that supplied the reservoir comes from a brook high in the Brecon Beacons. The quality of the water is believed to be vastly superior to the earlier supply.

Wellington Statue

The Wellington statue is the work of the celebrated sculptor John Thomas Evans, born at Brecon on 15 January 1810. The eldest son of John Thomas, of Castle Street, he studied in London and on the Continent and began to work independently in 1834. He became a frequent exhibitor at the Royal Academy between 1835 and 1857 during his very successful career, and many of his works are to be seen in Wales and elsewhere. Here in his home town, we have his statue of the Duke of Wellington standing proudly in the Bulwark. The statue was modelled from life and cast in bronze, mounted on a stone plinth adorned by bronzes plaques depicting various actions during the peninsular war. The cathedral holds more examples of his fine work. He died on 9 October 1873, in London where he is buried.

The Iron Duke, Brecon Bulwark, by John Thomas Evans, 2019. (Malcolm Morrison)

Wheat Street

Wheat Street is a short street where Brecon Coliseum stands proud, the lone survivor of Brecon's cinemas, which boasts that it has entertained Brecon for over ninety years (since 1925), showing the latest films to the people of the district. Other features

Wheat Street, 2019. (Malcolm Morrison)

worthy of our time are the Rorke's Drift Inn, formerly known as 'The Wheatsheaf', that may have given the street its name, and the ancient buildings of Buckingham Place at the Wheat Street/Glamorgan Street junction.

Woolworths

Every town of note once had a branch of F. W. Woolworth & Co. Brecon's store was located at No. 28 High Street Superior, next to today's NatWest bank. These stores were iconic, selling all manner of goods, very cheaply, including confectionery, clothing and electrical goods. One memory c. 1960 is of Woolworth's woollen swimwear, which was very popular for one season only. A 'wardrobe malfunction' occurred whenever the costume became wet, causing the lower part to sag alarmingly in a grotesquely hilarious manner!

The Brecon branch opened its doors in 1929 and continued to be a favourite of the public until its closure in December 2008.

Workhouse

In 1838, the Poor Law Commissioners approved an expenditure of £2,649 for a workhouse for 100 inmates. It has been suggested that the Llanfaes site was chosen as it was outside the town where the better-off would not have to see the paupers. The ground floor had workrooms, washrooms, a kitchen and rooms where new arrivals were stripped and cleansed. On the first floor were dormitories, staff quarters, the dining hall and rooms for the sick and infirm.

When a poor family was taken into the workhouse at Llanfaes they would be separated. The men were housed away from their wives and children and were only allowed to see them if the workhouse Master allowed. The inmates would be washed and given workhouse clothing and all their belongings taken from them. Life in the workhouse was harsh with no escape unless work outside could be found.

The 1861 Poor Law Board return identified twelve adult paupers who had been continuous workhouse inmates for five years or more. Three suffered from rheumatism, three were blind, three suffered old age, one had paralysis, one 'mental incapacity' and one suffered from dementia. An Alice Mills (rheumatism) had been there for fifteen years.

The master of the Union House in 1881 was thirty-six-year-old Henry Newman Kettle, whose wife, Mary, was Matron. They were assisted by nurse Sophia Banks and her husband George, whose occupation is given as House Porter. A Miss Rhoda Lawrence was employed as Industrial Trainer.

The 1881 census gives some insight into Victorian life. Forty-one of the workhouse inmates were children; the youngest, a Margaret Ann Bagley, was one years old.

Another inmate was nineteen-year-old Susan Bagley, an unmarried kitchen maid who very likely was the child's mother. Mary Jones, a seventy-seven-year-old blind harpist, seems to have been an inmate for over eighteen years! Labourers, kitchen maids and housemaids were the given occupations of many of the inmates, but several trades – shoemakers, joiners, carpenters, cooks and sailors – were recorded. Approximately one third of the residents were aged between sixteen and sixty.

Questions were asked in the House of Commons in 1913 regarding the number of children maintained in the Brecon workhouse as the guardians had been asked on three occasions what steps they were taking to secure the children's removal. They had replied that they were considering the question. However, members had openly stated their intention of doing nothing about the matter.

The minister, a strong critic of the workhouse system, replied that the number of children in this institution on 1 January 1913 was seventeen. The minister was asked if, under the circumstances, the Brecknock Union should be dissolved.

The workhouse eventually closed, and the building became St David's Hospital, providing care for geriatric patients. However, the fear and shame of the workhouse remained. One elderly lady, finding herself admitted to the hospital, begged her relatives to allow her home to die. She couldn't bear the thought of dying in the workhouse. She died contentedly in her own home a few days later.

The building has at least one ghost, a female who was regularly seen walking upstairs, and many St David's Hospital staff have claimed to have either seen or heard her, but she seems to be a friendly spirit as nothing untoward has so far been recorded.

One member of the staff discovered a tall cloaked figure in the day room in the small hours, and thinking it was an elderly confused patient, she asked what she was doing there. The figure rose from a kneeling position and stood over 6 feet tall

The former Brecon Workhouse, Bailiheleg Road, 2019. (Malcolm Morrison)

and moved towards the doorway on the stairs near the ward where a Mrs K*** was asleep. Suddenly all the bells in the building started ringing and the nurse shouted for her colleague who was taking a break. They timidly entered the ward and Mrs K*** was fully awake but very cross, complaining 'that awful woman has woken me again'. There was no sign of anyone else.

During another night, Sister T and the same nurse were in discussion, the Sister in the office doorway and the nurse across the corridor in the doorway of the staffroom. Suddenly they heard the door to the Day Hospital open and slam shut. They looked at each other in surprise and heard the sound of footsteps approaching from the Day Hospital to their corridor. The footsteps continued and 'walked' between them and turned into the day room. Sister T said it had happened before when she worked 'nights' but this was the only time another person also witnessed it.

A different lady saw somebody wearing a long grey dress and another time, as she was going down a flight of stairs carrying a bag of rubbish, 'a force of some kind stopped me for a moment or two'– she also recalled hearing the sound of breathing in an empty room. There were several reports of a 'presence' in the kitchen – feeling something brushing past or a strong feeling of a presence standing behind. The hospital closed in the early 1990s and the site was leased to Christ College for use as a hall of residence. Is this Brecon's most haunted building?

Watton

The origins of the name Watton, a road and once a ward of the town in times past, is tantalisingly difficult to uncover. An area with a similar name is the market town of Watton in the district of Breckland in Norfolk. The name Breckland apparently derives from a gorse-covered heath. I cannot help noticing an unlikely connection!

Another explanation is that Watton derives from an Old English 'wácor', meaning wicker or willow, and 'ton' meaning homestead or enclosure. This would fit with the Watton being an area near the river, having plenty of willow on its banks. Yet another explanation offered is that 'Watton' derives from the material that houses were built from in ancient times (i.e. daub and wattle).

A report into the sanitation of the town in 1847 stated that 'In the Watton there is what is called a sewer, which extends as far as the Barracks; it is really a reservoir for filth.' The area and many of the streets off it owe much to the coming of the canal. Many of these narrow streets began as canal wharfs that have since been filled in. The Watton itself is a wide, pretty tree-lined road with several inns and town houses along its way. The former assize courts that now forms part of Y Gaer (museum, library and art gallery) at the Watton Mount and the Barracks, with its impressive Keep, are the dominant features.

The road and area leading from the Watton towards today's Cerrigcochion Road were once known as Heol Rhydd Ward.

Above: The Peace Garden in the Watton, 2019. (Malcolm Morrison)

Below: Rich Way, the Watton, 2019. (Malcolm Morrison)

X – Division

X is a letter in our alphabet that has, in its own right, acquired several meanings. It can represent the signature of one unable to sign their name and it can represent a kiss in correspondence. The letter X is commonly used to abbreviate the word Christmas (Xmas), and the X Division was a Victorian term used to describe the criminal section of society. However, because of Brecon's traditional loyal and law-abiding demeanour, the term was never used hereabouts (written with fingers X'd). (Crossed fingers elicit good luck when making a wish or can forgive a 'white lie'.)

Painting]   CHARLES I. LEAVING PRIORY BRECON, AUGUST, 1645.   [*By Sam Garratt, N*

Charles I leaving Brecon Priory, August 1645. (Look and Learn Picture Library)

The letter X can also be an unknown quantity in a variety of situations including mathematics and it can also represent crossroads. Tir-y-groes, a small farm just beneath the Brecon Beacons, translates as 'the house at the cross'. Historians have argued about the use of the word groes; does it have religious connections or is it because ancient paths cross there? I prefer the crossroads version, but who knows? Groesffordd is another tiny village just outside town whose name literally means crossroads.

X – The Best of the Best

Brecon's most appropriate connection for the letter X is, I feel, the fact that X is the twenty-fourth letter of the modern English alphabet, and number 24 invokes much affection and respect here. I'm sure most readers will be well aware of the 24th Regiment, South Wales Borderers, until fairly recent times our local regiment. Various regimental amalgamations and government cuts have seen the gallant 24ths swallowed into today's Royal Welsh Regiment, but their history will never be forgotten. So many battle honours, so many Victoria Crosses won in every theatre of war and so many old soldiers who lived here in Brecon. Many of our grandparents served with this illustrious regiment and it has a dedicated chapel in our cathedral and a regimental museum, drawing visitors by the thousands.

X Marks the Spot

Voting in elections has traditionally been done by placing an X next to the name of the candidate one wishes to vote for. The results of parliamentary elections were traditionally announced from the steps of the Guildhall to huge crowds, and elections to the Brecon Town Council have been vigorously contested. Brecon is remembered for returning a female councillor in 1906/7, a lady who a few years later became the first lady mayor in the whole of Wales, and the second in the UK. She was a pioneer. Tudor Watkins will be remembered by many as our parliamentary representative during the 1950s and '60s; a very well-respected local man who now rests in the churchyard at Llanfaes. Known as a friend to the farmers, who made up a large part of the constituency, he always took great interest in local issues. He had an unusual way of speaking, sometimes missing out a letter in certain words, and adding an unnecessary letter in others. Was this 'parliamentary speak' from back in the day? I often wondered when he came to address us at school.

Y

Y Gaer (Roman Fortress)

Y Gaer is a substantial Roman fortress located a few miles north-east of the town. The site is well chosen: the earliest construction contained defensive banks with wooden palisades protecting the defenders. It was rebuilt in stone during the second century and at least some of the soldiers stationed at Y Gaer are known to have come from Spain. Some preservation work has recently been carried out, mainly to the gatehouse areas.

The fortress is under the care of CADW, but the farm and surrounding fields are private land. To get to Y Gaer from Brecon take the road to Cradoc village, then turn left to Aberyscir, making a left turn at the first crossroads (the site is not signposted); the road ends in a farmyard and Y Gaer is just beyond. It is rectangular with an entrance in the middle of each side. A substantial part of the perimeter wall with corner turrets is reasonably preserved, as are parts of a defensive ditch. Much of the foundations of the gates and guardrooms survive and recent archaeological preservation work has taken place. Earlier excavations have uncovered many interesting artefacts, some of which are on view at Brecon museum. It does seem odd that we know more about this Roman fortress than the Norman castle in the centre of our town.

Y Gaer Roman fortress. (Malcolm Morrison)

Y Gaer (Brecon Museum, Art Gallery and Library)

As I write, a new hub comprising Brecon's library, museum and art gallery is about to open its doors to visitors. This exciting venture brings together three vital components of a modern, forward-looking town. The construction work has revolved around the old county assize court building with a new and well-designed annexe to welcome visitors into its heart. As is usual with a major construction project, this venture has suffered delays and disappointments and has come in for more than its share of undeserved and sometimes hysterical negative publicity. Perhaps the people of Brecon will delay further judgment until its doors open so that a balanced view can be given. I suspect they will be pleasantly surprised.

Front view of 'Y Gaer', Brecon's library, art gallery and museum, 2019. (Malcolm Morrison)

Rear view of 'Y Gaer', Brecon's exciting new cultural hub, 2019. (Malcolm Morrison)

Z

Zulu Wars

The Zulu War Room at the regimental museum of the Royal Welsh in the Watton focuses on the exploits of the 24th Regiment during the 1879 Anglo-Zulu Wars. At the time of the wars, the 24th Regiment's home base was Brecon and from the regimental rolls it is clear that the regiment had a significant Welsh base, particularly at Rorke's Drift. It also seems that the events on the African veldt in 1879 would haunt the men for years to come. The story of the slaughter of the British forces at Isandlwana on 21 January and the subsequent heroic defence at Rorke's Drift over 22–23 January is well known and doesn't require retelling here, but Private Henry Hook wrote to his mother, 'Every man fought dearly for his life. We were all determined to sell our lives like soldiers and to keep up the credit of our regiment.'

The wars fought 140 years ago have forged close links between the Zulu nation in Kwazulu and Brecon. Former enemies now warmly welcome each other with mutual respect. The most recent visit was in July 2019, the highlight of which was a regiment of Zulu warriors deployed in 1879 regalia with assegais, shields and leopard skin headgear dancing and singing their historic war chants along the Watton as they approached the barracks, their blood-curdling songs and war dances setting the scene for a most colourful pageant.

Zulu warrior, Brecon Barracks, July 2019. (Andrew Williams)

Zulu warriors performing traditional war dance, The Watton, 2019. (Andrew Williams)

Zymotic Disease

Zymotic disease is an old medical term for acute infectious diseases such as typhus, typhoid fever, smallpox, cholera and diphtheria. Over a five-year period during the 1840s, zymotic disease is recorded as the second biggest cause of death in Brecon town with almost one fifth of all reported deaths attributed to it.

The exact causes of the epidemics that recurred with alarming regularity were not understood at the time, but it became obvious that they were focused upon specific areas of town, usually the areas where poorer families lived: 'The nuisances arising from the seven pig sty's at Kensington ... the filth at the side of the public footpath in Mill Street leading to Newton Pool and ... the filthy state of Silver Street, Beech Street and Walnut-row in Llanfaes' came in for particular criticism. 'There are very many cottages that have no privies, many no outlet at the back, and filth of every kind is too often thrown before the doors to the disadvantage of the public, and there allowed to accumulate,' reported George Thomas Clark in a scathing report into the water and sanitary conditions in 1849. The sewerage system was extremely poor and much of the town relied upon rainfall and regular flooding by the rivers to cleanse its thoroughfares. Parts of the town had natural drainage due to the slopes down towards the rivers but Llanfaes, being flat, relied almost entirely upon flooding to cleanse its streets. We can only speculate about the ambience of our beloved town during hot summers.

Eventually the connection between polluted drinking water and contagious diseases was made and a proper system of sewerage and water supply was established, with public health improving immediately.

Note – The biggest killer at the time was lung disease (25 per cent), which included pulmonary tuberculosis, pneumonia and bronchitis. Diseases affecting the brain and spinal marrow, nerves and senses came third, accounting for 147 (17 per cent), with deaths from 'old age' the fourth biggest killer with 137 cases (16 per cent). Disease of the heart and blood vessels killed just 21 (2.4 per cent), which is perhaps surprising as currently this is the biggest cause of death.

Acknowledgements

So many people have helped with the production of this book that is difficult to know where to begin. Very special thanks to my wife Sue for her encouragement, suggestions and help with the manuscript; to Jill and Rosie Bright for their excellent suggestions and help with the manuscript; to the staff at Brecon Library for use of the microfiche; the *Brecon and Radnor Express* for recording so much of Brecon's history; Wynne Rees for photographs and information on the gather; special thanks to Andrew (Will) Williams for his photographs, help and forgiveness (he will understand); Roger Barrington for some fantastic documents; and Jonathan Williams for photographs and information. To Mrs Doris Tilley; Keith Williams (Brecon RFC); Barrie Lowe Adele Evans and Noreen Richards for the photos; Steve Morris for his valuable help; and Karen Thomas, Mike Peters, Sian Vaughan, Wendy Goode, Deanna Leboff, Jenny Aulsebrook, and Owen Williams for some great ghost stories. Most importantly, thanks to Jenny Stephens and everybody at Amberley Publishing, without whose support this book would never have happened.

For any error or omission, I can only apologise, but everything is offered in good faith. Permissions have been sought for all photographs used – the majority are from my own collection or camera – however, if I have overlooked someone or accidentally omitted thanks or acknowledgement, I can only offer my sincere apologies and will endeavour to correct at the first opportunity.

Other Sources

Anon, <http://www.childrenshomes.org.uk/BreconWS/ - Dinas Orphanage>

Anon, *Infantry Battle School* <https://www.army.mod.uk/who-we-are/our-schools-and-colleges/infantry-battle-school>

Anon, *The British Military Open Encyclopaedia* - ARRSE-Podia, <https://www.arrse.co.uk/wiki/Dering_Lines> Anone, *Hereford Journal,* Saturday 4 January 1845

Brown, R. L. 'One of the most remarkable men of his time', *Brycheiniog* (2002, v.XXXIV) pp. 119/131

Edwards, F., Some Recollections of Early Llandrindod Wells, *Radnorshire Society Transactions* v.62, p. 95

Goodall, P. J. R., *Ring the Bell in the Gaols of Brecon* (Gwasg Carreg Gwalch, 2006) Carradice, p., <https://www.bbc.co.uk/blogs/waleshistory/2011/01/anglo_zulu_wars_1879.html>

Jenkins, R.T., *Jones, Theophilus (1759-1812), the historian of Brecknock*, Dictionary of Welsh Biography, Bangor, 1959 <https://biography.wales/article/s-JONE-THE> <http://historypoints.org/index.php?page=rhys-ap-thomas-effigy-carmarthen> <https://thetudorchronicles.wordpress.com/2015/08/22/on-this-day-in-1485-battle-of-bosworth> <http://historypoints.org/index.php?page=in-memory-of-richard-aveline-maybery>

Jones, T., *History of the County of Brecknock* (Edwin Davies, 1898 ed.)

Kelleher, Sr. B., Theatre in Brecon in the 18th & 19th Century, *Brycheiniog* (1993 v.XXV) pp.79-80 Morgan, J., *Famous Figures of Christ College Brecon* (Cambria Publishing, 2018) Parri, B., Some Problematic Place-names in Breconshire, *Brycheiniog* (2002, v.XXXIV) pp. 57/8

Poole, E., *The Illustrated History and Biography of Brecknockshire* (Edwin Poole, 1886) Powell, R. F. P., Early Place-names in the former Borough of Brecknock, *Brycheiniog* (1993, v.XXV) pp. 21/25

Reed, Keith, *Cromwell's March Through Neath* <http://www.spanglefish.com/neathheritage/index.asp?pageid=429294>

UK Office for National Statistics

Wright, H. G. <https://biography.wales/article/s-VAUG-HEN-1621>